Kip's Tips

KIP ROSENTHAL, PhD

Kip's Tips

iUniverse books may be ordered through booksellers or by contacting:

iUniverse
1663 Liberty Drive
Bloomington, IN 47403
www.iuniverse.com
1-800-Authors (1-800-288-4677)

ISBN: 978-1-5320-8140-8 (sc)
978-1-5320-8141-5 (e)

Library of Congress Control Number: 2019912745

Print information available on the last page.

iUniverse rev. date: 06/19/2020

Kip's Tips

CONTENTS

Chapter 1   FLAT RIDING 1

Chapter 2   JUMPING 21

Chapter 3   HORSE SHOWS 45

Chapter 4   PSYCHOLOGY ISSUES 59

Chapter 5   OTHER QUESTIONS..69

INTRODUCTION

I was extremely fortunate growing up that my parents were very supportive and I had great teachers. My first riding experience began at Fox Hill Farms in Pleasantville, New York, when I was ten. There, under the guidance of Ann and Frank Grenci, I learned my true love of horses. It was a very caring, nurturing, family-oriented business. Weekends and summers, I was dropped off at the barn in the early morning and stayed late as a true "barn rat". I would do anything to help and had a wonderful time there for three and a half years.

When it was time to move on to a barn that showed a bit more competitively on a national level, I went to Cedar Lodge Farm in Stamford, Connecticut and rode with Victor Hugo-Vidal. Although he sold me my first wonderful horse, Goodboy Dee, and I was quite successful, I'm afraid I don't remember many good/fun times. I guess that you could say I learned how not to teach. Victor was a brilliant teacher, but his system was taught through intimidation and sometimes fear.

After a year and a half there, I went to George Morris. He was my teacher, mentor, and now a great friend. George is the one who always encouraged me to teach from the time I was young. Quite frankly, I can't say enough good about George. He is a genius! Just look at all the grand prix riders he has taught and the many riders and assistants who have gone on to become trainers themselves. No matter what you may have heard about George's reputation, he was always demanding but fair. He was tyrannical about having a system, complete preparation for both horse and rider, integrity, and unequaled self-discipline. For this I will always be grateful. One of the best times I had with George was when we both judged the 2002 AHSA Medal Finals. My teacher, mentor, and great friend had and become my co-judge! I am the teacher that I am today because of George's influence, and for that I am eternally grateful.

I rode with George until I went to college, and then I met up with him at the horse shows. After my junior years, I rode with several other people who helped shape me as a solid horsewoman. I went to Bennett College and rode with Carol (nee Molony) and Jim Fallon. I had a great time there; riding became fun again after many grueling years on the "A" show circuit. As much as I loved showing and being very successful, I don't think I could possibly show today without going home to practice and giving my horses some much-needed breaks.

I was blessed with the opportunity to study with several important trainers before I became a professional. One was United States Equestrian Team show jumping coach Bert de Nemethy, who taught me the importance of flatwork without gimmicks. I learned how to "sit zee trot" (in Bert's Hungarian accent) and prepare jumpers to be reactive to aids as well as learning suppleness and straightness, all through specific exercises and gymnastics. Spending time at the team headquarters at Gladstone was a remarkable experience.

Thanks to Dave Kelly, with whom I spent a winter in Southern Pines, North Carolina, I learned how to "break" (saddle and bridle) youngsters. Dave was wonderful with young horses, a part of the sport in which I had no real experience. He didn't have a ring, but there was a huge beautiful field with all kinds of jumps. However, Dave always started the three- and four-year-old's jumping out on the trails. Either Dave or I would ride an experienced horse while the other was aboard the baby. We played "elephants in a circus:" by following the older horse over small "natural" jumps. When the baby could lead the experienced horse without any fears, we brought them into the home field to jump. What a great introduction! I never remember any fear with Dave's horses. He was meticulous in the barn and worked right along with his employees in feeding, mucking, turning out, and all the other chores. He was a great horseman!

The last person who was so instrumental before I turned professional was Frances Rowe. She lived in Virginia, and I went to Florida with her as an amateur. Francis knew *every* detail about every horse under her care. To her, each horse was an individual and needed a specific program to peak at the right moment. She had some of the greatest grand prix jumpers in the country, with Conrad Homfeld, Joe Fargis and Joan Boyce as her riders. Can you imagine the chance to watch those people ride and train every day? It was classic horsemanship (I never saw a bamboo pole, offset or tack rail on her property). She was a genius in preparing a horse to "win" a particular class. She was very thorough on conditioning and keeping her horses healthy and happy. Her employees stayed with her for years. (I, too, have had the same marvelous employees for two decades because I learned from Frances that "a great horseman is only as great as the sum of his its parts.") Frances's achievement was amazing in that very few women in the early- to mid-1970's had as much success as she did. It was more of a man's world, at least from my point of view. I thank Frances for showing me, that if I worked hard enough, I could be as successful as she in this field that I loved.

Growing up I was a very average student. However, certain tests I took showed that I could do much better. I tried to be a better student and I knew I was working as hard as I could, but I basically fell through the cracks. Obviously back in the sixties there was no such thing as dyslexia or reading/learning difficulties. I was *very* fortunate my parents never threatened to take riding away from me until I received better grades. But I knew I tried as hard as I could, so how did I feel about myself? *Stupid.* However, during that time in high school, I was very fortunate that I was very successful in the show ring with two wonderful horses at two different times. That's what kept me going!

During the eighties, I was conducting a clinic in New Jersey and became friends with a participant named Dale Huebner. During a conversation I told her I didn't know if I could read. She was an LDTC (learning disabilities specialist) and reading consultant. She actually took her time to teach me how to read. She opened up the world to me! I decided to test my new knowledge and went back to college part-time to finish my bachelor's degree in psychology. Then I was eager to learn more. So, I went on and received two Master's degrees in education and psychology. I was beginning to feel better about myself. I was teaching riding, conducting clinics and judging part-time, as well as going to school. This taught me time management skills. From this experience I went on to obtain a Doctoral degree in Adolescent Clinical Psychology. There was no such degree as Sports Psychology as there is today. However, I felt that with the knowledge I had in education and psychology, combined with many years of riding and teaching, I could develop my own system of sports psychology.

All of these experiences in riding and academia have shaped my life with horses and my love of teaching. I had a business called Benchmark Farms for many years and now spend more time conducting sports psychology seminars at many schools, farms and universities, as well as private sessions. With such a background as mine, you wouldn't be surprised to hear that I never stop learning. To this day I always try to find out what I *don't* know. I still listen, watch, and ask questions from the many people I respect.

The musical show, *The King and I*, has the line, "When you become a teacher, by your pupils you'll be taught." That's been the case throughout my teaching career. I've been blessed with decades of students who, in George Morris's words, learned to see, and not just look, and to listen, and not just hear. My best students have been sponges, eager to soak up as much information as they can and then work through the "muddling period" (about which you'll read in these pages) to apply their new skills, many of which become the building blocks for more advanced skills. Horsemanship is a never-ending process of problem-solving made more difficult---but also more fulfilling---because the rider's "equipment" is another living creature.

This book came out of a series of question-and-answers columns that I have written for *Equestrian Today* magazine. Since I received many "repeat" questions, I listened to friends who suggested compiling the columns in book form. Where I saw "holes" or remembered questions that my students and others asked, I added them to the text.

I hope you find this book useful. Happy learning and happy riding!

CHAPTER 1

FLAT RIDING

The function of a correct position is to produce correct aids.

As a rider, your eyes make the first commitment on where you're going and help maintain the rider's balance. The rider should sit evenly on both sitting bones and stay within the horse's motion. The only time a rider should *not* move is when the horse is at a halt or standing still. Once the horse is moving, the rider has to move with the horse. If a rider tries to sit still when the horse is moving, it will create a stiff rider and hollow horse.

In short, a good seat is balanced, relaxed, and flexible.

When I look at a rider, I look at the whole picture. Then the first part of the body my eyes go to is the lower legs, ankles, and heels. It's similar to the basement in a house. If it's insecure, the building will collapse and so will the rider! The rider's legs need to be long, with the ankles flexed down and in, allowing the heels to drop. This is the rider's anchor; if the horse is strong and can pull the rider out of the saddle, he or she is at the horse's mercy. The weight of the rider's stirrups should be held on the inside branch; this allows the rider's weight to deepen into the stirrup and will stabilize the rider's legs. The lower leg is the accelerator. It's the part of the rider's body that moves the horse longitudinally (forward and backward), as well as laterally (side to side). The rider's thighs and seat are the rider's base of support. They need to be down and yet remain supple. The seat can be used as both a driving aid and a resisting aid.

The rider's hands should be on the same angle as the horse's withers. This allows the rider's hands and arms to ride the entire length of their horse. Flat hands only allow the rider to ride the front end of the horse. Warning: when you see top hunter riders and/or grand prix riders ride with flat hands, this is *not* what makes them great; it is idiosyncratic that has made them great. I believe hands and fingers are, the most difficult part of the riders' bodies, that truly makes them advanced riders. Arms and hands basically control the front end of horses and legs create impulsion to ride the back end. It takes years and years of practice to learn how to coordinate those aids to communicate with horses.

Q. How do I teach my students the correct hand position and correct use of their hands?

A. I can certainly tell you how to teach correct hand position but teaching riders how to use their hands correctly is, in my opinion, the most difficult thing to learn… and only very advanced riders truly know correct hand usage. It's an ongoing process, one where we're constantly communicating with our horses' mouths. Just know that unless you're getting run off with, your hand aids should *never* be stronger than your leg aids!

For teaching correct hand position, if a rider is able to carry a stick/crop in both hands and place the stick mid-thigh, it will automatically put the rider's hand in the correct position on that horse. Just make sure the rider's wrists are straight and all ten fingers are closed, yet soft. Their hands should be carried just above and just in front of their horse's withers. There will probably be very little variation from horse to horse in hand position. The hands should be kept about the width of the bit unless using different specific rein aids, such as an opening rein when the hands will be further apart, or an indirect rein when the hands might be a little closer together. Teach your riders to keep their shoulders relaxed and their elbows supple and to follow their horse's stride at all gaits so they learn how to ride with their horse rather than against their horse's motion. The reason this hand position is important is when riders get to a more advanced level, perhaps in jumper riding, more advanced equitation or higher-level dressage, the rider wants to be able to influence the length of their horse. It becomes important that the rider has a straight line from the horse's mouth through the rider's fingers and fists to their elbows. Then the rider's arms act like pendulums, and they are able to connect their horse's back ends to the rider's hands to the horse's mouth. Riding back to front... is a very advanced concept. But if you teach your riders the correct hand position, you'll establish a correct riding habit. It takes years and years to learn to develop "feel" and maintain a meaningful conversation with your horse's mouth!

Q. How can I teach my riders the correct leg position?

A. I start at the rider's heels and ankles. The outside branch of the stirrup (closer to the inside of the ring) should be "slightly" ahead of the inside stirrup branch. This will allow her to put more weight on the inside part of her foot and allow her ankle to flex down and in, and in turn, drop her weight into her heels. This creates a brace, an anchor against the horse's pull. If her weight is on the outside of her foot, her leg will be pulled away from the horse's side. Her heels and ankles act as the foundation of a building, similar to a basement. The foundation must be strong for the building to remain upright.

The calves are the rider's accelerators. They should always be in contact with the horse's sides. As riders advance, their legs will become more educated and elastic and seem to breathe with their horses. The calves would be comparable to the first floor in a house.

The riders' thighs are their base of support. Riders should have about equal amounts of weight distributed between their thighs, inner knee bones and calves.

Q. What's a good exercise to get my students' base of support stronger?

A. Well, the best one that comes to my mind first is riding without stirrups, both on the flat and jumping. When jumping, start with very small jumps, such as cross rails and maybe just a two-foot and two-foot-six-inch verticals. Hold off on oxers until you think your riders are strong enough in their base and aren't using their horses' mouths for balance. Make sure you take the stirrups off their saddles, so they aren't hitting their horses' sides. Also, don't cross them over their horses' withers because they could potentially hit the rider in their face! Once they are secure in their legs and thighs, then add oxers into your jumps. Just know it's harder to maintain balance over oxers. So again, start small and narrow and widen the oxers and make them bigger as your riders get tighter and hold their balance with their bodies and not their horses' mouths.

Q. My horse ignores my leg sometimes. He'll respond a stride or two later, or not at all. How do I make him more responsive?

A. You are your horse's trainer. You have to decide how sensitive you want your horse to be to your aids. This is *not* your horse's choice!

When you use your legs either to go forward or move laterally, the horse must respond immediately yet in a relaxed manner. Use your legs first. If you don't get the response you want immediately, use your spurs or your stick. When using artificial aids, you need to get an over response. You don't want to rely on these aids for your horse to respond.

Once your horse responds to these aids, bring your horse back to the original gait and go back to your natural aid: your leg pressure. Repeat this exercise until your horse responds to your leg aids. Increase your artificial aids until your horse understands what you want either longitudinally or laterally.

It's extremely important that you are very consistent with your aids, and your horse will soon respond to your leg pressure. It is a process called conditioning. You apply an aid, and your horse either responds correctly or does not. If he does, then relax your aid. This is his reward. If he doesn't, then increase your aids, using either spurs or a crop, until your horse understands your aids.

If you're consistent it won't take long for your horse to understand your leg aids.

Q. I just got a new student whose horse is really dead to the leg. She keeps kicking him and kicking him and he just ignores her. How do I teach the horse to be responsive to her leg?

A. It is important that a horse is responsive to a rider's aids, especially if the rider plans to jump. Kicking is dangerous and unproductive. It is dangerous because it takes the rider's leg off the horse and the rider loses connection to the horse. Also, the horse will only become more "dead" to the leg as time goes by.

The rider must learn how to use an artificial aid, either spurs or a riding stick, to train the horse to be responsive to the rider's legs. If the rider's leg is correct and steady in position, then teach the student how to use spurs to educate the horse to the rider's legs. The correct implementation of aids is: The rider first squeezes her leg to ask the horse to move forward. If the horse is dull and doesn't immediately react, then she gives the horse a quick jab with spurs and gets an overreaction. Then the rider "squeezes" the horse back with normal leg pressure and again asks the horse to move forward only using leg pressure.

If the horse responds correctly, great! If not, the rider once again uses her spurs more vigorously to get an overreaction, then again returns to just leg pressure. It is important to get an overreaction; otherwise the rider is training the horse to listen and react to the spurs, not her rider's leg!

Q. Some of my students have a hard time learning how to pick up their diagonals. Do you have any suggestions on how to teach them to correctly pick them up?

A. It's funny, usually riders can pick up the correct diagonal in one direction almost 100 percent of the time, and yet miss one in the other direction. Why, who knows?

My suggestion is that the rider start at the sitting trot and try to "feel" which front leg is going first, then sit a beat and begin to post. The rider shouldn't look down but try to feel if she is correct. If she isn't sure, she should change to the other diagonal and see if this one feels better, then glance down to check. Usually if a rider tries this approach, in time she will begin to pick up the correct diagonal more often.

With riders who absolutely cannot pick up the correct diagonal, I would tie a ribbon around the horse's outside front leg and have the rider begin to post when she sees the ribbon going forward. Then have the rider notice the horse's shoulder going forward, until she can feel one shoulder versus the other. But most importantly, once the rider picks up one diagonal, allow time for her to feel it and then change to the other diagonal until she can tell one from the other. Don't make this into a big deal. In time, all riders will figure out the correct diagonal.

Q. My horse is very crooked to the left. He just turns his head way to the inside and goes with his head cocked sideways. I thought his teeth were bothering him and had them done (they were pretty bad), but that hasn't helped. How can I straighten him out?

A. My first question concerns when the dentist worked on your horse. If it was a short time ago, it's very possible that your horse's mouth (inside cheeks) are still sore from sharp teeth. If not, is this a new behavior? If it is, then I would have your vet come out and check him. I'd ask your vet to draw some blood and do a CBC chemistry, an EPM, and a Lyme titer. Always rule out any physical problems with your vet if your horse's normal behavior has changed.

That being said and assuming your horse is perfectly healthy, then we have to go to some training exercises. It's very important that when you ride your horse, you start off with an engine. What I mean by this is that he is in front of your legs. Don't pay attention to his head and neck; just make sure he is going forward from your legs. Next, teach him to go from your inside leg to your outside hand. That will help get your horse straight. If he's just tipping his nose in and not really bending, you *must* push him from your inside leg to your outside hand.

Every time he tries to evade your aids, then you need *more* inside leg. Just remember that with every ounce of hand aid, you need two ounces of leg (at least)! It sounds as though your horse is not on your outside hand. Once he's going forward and if he's reluctant to go on to your outside hand, a good exercise is a shoulder-in.

Your horse will always be better in one direction than the other, but as trainers, we try to get our horses as comfortable, supple, strong, and confident going in both directions.

Q. I just switched to a new trainer, and the new trainer keeps telling me to half-halt. I don't really understand what a half-halt is or what it does. Could you explain it to me?

A. A half-halt is a way to rebalance or reconnect your horse from his front end to his back end. When your horse gets heavy on his front end and his carriage becomes long and low, it is an aid to "lift" your horse's balance up and back.

You use your hands, seat, and legs to achieve a momentary rebalancing, or a signal to prepare your horse for a change of gait or pace. You accomplish this aid by resisting your horse with both your hands and seat while maintaining his impulsion with both your legs. This is all done within one stride. You will probably have to repeat a series of half-halts many times before your horse becomes light.

Remember, it is important that you keep your horse going *forward* through the half-halts. If you use too much hand without your legs, your horse will just become heavier and lay more on your hands.

Once your horse understands this aid, he will not rely on your hands to hold his weight up. The half-halt is a very important aid that you both need to learn so your horse learns how to carry his own weight and stay light in your hands.

Any exercise that deals with lateral exercise, such as circles, serpentines, broken lines, figure eights and shoulder-ins/outs will help supple your horse.

Q. My horse is very stiff, and I would like to make her more supple. What exercises would you suggest? Thanks!

A. Stiff horses need to do a lot of lateral exercises to get them supple so they can go straight. A crooked horse is a stiff horse.

A great exercise for stiffness is the following: Put your horse on a circle about thirty meters at the walk. If you are tracking right, bend him to the left and push his haunches to the right. Make the circles incrementally smaller until your circle is very small. Then bend him to the right and push his haunches to the left. You want his right hind leg to cross over his left hind leg.

Once he can do this at the walk, then go to a posting trot. When the circle becomes fairly small, sit the trot to help him stay engaged. Then do this exercise at the canter.

Do this exercise in both directions. It's a great way to get your horse supple while working both ends of your horse. Your hands control the front end (head, neck, and shoulders) while your legs control your horse's hind end (haunches). Take your time with this exercise, and your horse will become much more supple.

Q. What is the differences between collection and going slower and extension and going faster? What do the extended and collected strides look like?

A. Okay, the basic difference in the question you've asked is speed versus impulsion. Slow and fast is exactly that … they involve speed. Collection and extension involve impulsion. Impulsion comes from the horse's back legs; it's his form of energy. The three joints of the horse's hind legs are his fetlocks, hocks, and stifles all have to work much stronger in both collection and extension than in speed. Then with your horse's energy (impulsion), the rider can shorten the horse's stride to be very "lively" and short thus in collection or allow the horse's stride to lengthen, which becomes an extended stride. In the photos you'll see the difference between the collected and extended strides.

Q. My horse has a VERY long stride, which is wonderful. However, I can't seem to find a way to shorten it. There is no elasticity to his stride… it's always long. Do you have any exercises that I can try to be able to adjust his stride?

A. I have a wonderful exercise for teaching horses how to elasticize their stride. I start with three ground poles an equal distance apart. I like the distance to be a "nice loose" four strides. If you have a way to measure, it (a one hundred feet measure reel is a great tool to have in your barn) will probably be anywhere from fifty eight to sixty feet. But adjust it so your horse, can canter the poles in four loose relaxed strides between the three poles.

Begin by cantering and ride your horse in an even four strides between the three poles. Then collect the stride so your horse can do five strides. It's important that if your horse tries to do four strides, you stop him and do not allow him to do four strides. The object is to get your horse to relax and put in five strides. Once you can canter the three poles in four or five strides, then canter in in five strides and canter out in four strides. Your horse needs to be relaxed for the five strides so that on the last step, you are able to relax and begin to open his stride to continue out in four steps.

This will become easy in time. Then ask him to canter the first two poles in four strides and collect for five strides between the last two poles. If he tries to do four, stop him *before* he does the four!

Once you can adjust your horse's stride to work between four and five strides, he will be more elastic in his stride. Then you might do this same exercise over three small jumps. You'll need to adjust the distances to keep the four loose strides. The main objective is to keep the poles/jumps at the same distance so you can teach him how to lengthen and shorten his stride.

Be patient, and he will learn how to become more adjustable and elastic. The continuation of the exercise is his reward

When riding your horse, you'll need to do a lot of transitions both within the gait and between gaits. You need to ride him forward, then collect him. He needs to be prompt in both forward and collected transitions.

If your horse lays on your hands in a downward transition, give him a half-halt, which will rebalance his weight from his front end to his back end. A half-halt is a smooth uptake of your horse's mouth with your hands and using your legs added at the same time. It will shift his weight from his front end to his back end. It rebalances your horse. Again, do this both within the trot and again When riding your horse, you'll need to do a lot of transitions both within the gait and between gaits. You need to ride him forward, then collect him. He needs to be prompt in both forward and collected transitions.

You'll have to be very diligent in doing these transitions. Repetition … Repetition … Repetition. Be patient but firm and you can teach your horse how to connect his back end to his front end. It's always a function of back to front in your ride.

Q. I took a clinic, and the clinician told me that my horse is "right-handed." What exactly does that mean, and how do I fix it?

A. All horses are one-sided as are most people! Horses don't drop out of the womb any more ambidextrous than humans. I believe that the clinician may have said that your horse is right-handed, meaning that he is more supple on the right side. That means that your horse is better going to the right than the left. If this is correct, then I would always start working your horse to the right first, his better direction.

Once you've worked your horse to the right, then you need to do suppling exercises to the left to try and strengthen his left side. To supple and strengthen the left side, I would do a lot of lateral exercises. These exercises would include circles, shoulder-in, haunches in, and broken lines-all exercises to supple and strengthen your horse's left side. You want your horse to stay calm and relaxed. Repeat exercises, but don't drill his left side until he becomes annoyed or frustrated.

Remember, you have to introduce these exercises in a calm, patient way. Work your horse in both directions. When going to the left, his harder way, if you feel he is trying to go back to the right, be sure to let him take a breath and relax.

Q. My young horse is just starting to learn flying changes. My problem is every time I try to go thru the middle of the ring, he tries to do a flying change. If I hold him so he doesn't anticipate the change, he becomes tense and starts to hop up and down. Help please, I don't want to discourage him since he's just learned the change, but do you have any suggestions for me?

A. This is a difficult situation. I *never* allow my horses to do lead changes on the center line across the diagonal, nor in the middle of the ring. My horses must hold their lead until the far quarter or second quarter line, even if it involves holding the counter canter until the horse waits to be told to change his lead.

If your horse anticipates a lead change as he goes across the ring, turn him in the direction of the lead you are on and just make a circle. If he swaps his lead before you circle, do a *simple* lead change and continue to circle on the lead you are currently on.

You always want your horse to anticipate what you want but *wait* to be told. This can be very challenging, but if you take your time and stay calm, you can get your horse to wait to be told to change his lead.

Q. How do you teach your riders different speeds at the canter?

A. The canter is usually about ten to twelve miles per hour. But you can use arbitrary numbers, just so you can teach your riders a slow canter and a faster canter. Advanced riders learn the working, extended, and collected canters, but beginner and intermediate riders should be taught speeds rather than length of strides. Your riders can learn speeds in a ring or on a field. If you're in a field, just give them the idea of riding with two long sides and two short sides, as though they were in a ring. You can even use cones, blocks, or cavalettis to "map out" your boundaries.

I find that a lot of riders tend to ride a canter slower than the one they'll need for jumping. So, when they jump, they're not comfortable working with more speed. I'll give you flat and jumping exercises I use to teach them two different speeds. I'll start off having them go at a faster canter (twelve mph) on the long side of the ring/field and then slow their speed (ten mph)

on the short side. Then I'll mix it up and have them go faster on the short side and slower on the long side. Have them demonstrate to you that they understand the two different speeds.

Set up a small vertical and tell them to jump the fence a total of four times, two times on both leads, once at ten mph and again at twelve mph. Once you feel they understand the two speeds, set two jumps in a row with a related distance. Obviously, the footage will be different for ponies and horses. And the distance will ride differently for longer and shorter horses/ponies. But see if you can set up the two jumps so that when going faster, they can ride the line in one less stride, and the same line with the slower canter in one more stride. If you're in a big ring or a field and the horses have about the same stride length, then I'd probably set the distance about seventy-five feet if the jump is about two feet six inches. That should ride in a quite forward five strides or a very steady six strides. You might have to play around with the footage depending on horses and/or ponies. If they're all together, you can normally just add one more stride for the ponies. When I go to shows with my pre child/adult riders, I'll explain the course to them in terms of the speed they'll need for the different lines. Especially if a line is used twice and how that will probably have to be ridden at twelve mph as the first line and ten mph as the last line. I just find this a good way to teach my beginner and novice riders the different speeds they'll need for pretty basic courses.

Q. I have a student who seems to have too strong a seat. She drives her horse crazy; he goes around inverted and keeps getting quicker. How do I help her achieve a lighter seat?

A. Some horses' backs are more sensitive than others. Make sure the horse's saddle fits properly, which might be the problem. Also, a horse with a sore back may require medication or a veterinarian's help or both.

If this is not the issue, the horse might just be super-sensitive, or the rider's seat is too strong. I suggest you try this exercise. When she picks up her canter, have her get in two-point jumping position. Have her slowly sink down into the saddle and feel how much pressure her horse can handle until he becomes tense, quick, or strong.

Some horses' backs are super-sensitive, and the rider must acknowledge, accept, and work with that. You can't change a horse's sensitivity level, so the rider must change her seat pressure. Sometimes a rider's seat needs to be so light that it is as though she were sitting on a

porcupine. In cases like this, the only contact the horse will accept is the pressure of the rider's riding pants.

Next, have your student do the exercise I've suggested until the rider understands the amount of pressure her horse can withstand. She must learn to find her balance and ride off her legs rather than from her horse's back. The horse will be very appreciative that she is trying to accommodate his sensitivity.

Q. I have a cute young mare that is rather long backed. I feel as though I am riding two different horses, with the front end and the hind end not connected. What can I do to connect her two ends?

A. First of all, I appreciate the fact you recognize that *both* the back end as well as the front end need to connect. I see so much draw-rein riding, which leads me to think that many people are only interested in their horse's front end. Obviously draw reins can be a great training aid in very educated hands! I never really learned how to use draw reins, so I stay away from them in my training. Sometimes I'll use them on the sides of the horse to help with straightness but never between the horse's front legs.

Let me say that I have short legs, so I hate it when the horse is strong, heavy, and long. So, whereas many people try to get the horse's head down to connect, I do just the opposite! I want the horse's head high, no matter how disconnected. This allows me to use *a lot* of leg to engage his motor (back end). Horses can't buck, pull, or drag when their heads are up, and I don't have enough leverage to try and connect both ends at once. I will use a series of half halts along with strong legs to keep the horse's head up. Then I'll do transitions within the walk, trot, and canter, as well as between the three gaits. Next, I work on straightness of track. Most horses are crooked and stiff. You need to feel which side is stiffer. Ask yourself while riding, "Where are my horse's haunches in relation to his front end?" Then start doing lateral exercises, such as circles, half turns, and other patterns that will get your horse more supple.

Do *not* worry about head carriage other than that his head needs to be high so he can't pull! Once you have your horse's head high, going forward, and (reasonably) straight, then you can *allow* him to lower his head. Then start again with a lot of transitions.

These exercises will enable you to create the connection you want and an elastic stride. If and when your horse becomes disconnected, and it *will* happen again, don't worry; just go back to the earlier steps. Learning is a process, and it takes time for your horse to learn and become consistent. Just remember that connection starts with your legs engaging and straightening his hind end and your hands monitoring his front end in regard to pace, stride, and rhythm.

Q. My horse seems to be two separate animals: one in front and one in back. There is no connection in between. How do I get him to be connected and come from behind?

A. There are a few things you can do to get your horse connected from back to front. One would be to buy a Pessoa lunging rig, or you can see how the device is made and buy the "ropes" at Home Depot! Essentially, it's a device that goes from the outside of your horse through a ring on a surcingle to the near (inside) around his back end, with the rope padded behind his hindquarters through a ring on the near side through the bit to a second lunge line. You can see a picture of this in most tack shop catalogue or on a website.

This way, from the ground you can help your horse connect his back end to his front end. It will require you to handle two lunge lines and a lunge whip. Obviously, your horse has to know how to lunge before you can use this rig.

Now stand and face your horse's side and picture him as if you'd lopped off his head and neck. Would his shape be a square or a rectangle? If his body shape looks like a square, it'll be pretty easy to coordinate his back end to his front end. However, if his body shape looks more like a rectangle it will be a little harder, but you can certainly teach him how to be more connected from back to front.

CHAPTER 2

JUMPING

Q. What are the basic seat positions you teach your riders?

A. I teach five seat positions, although two are more extreme. Normally we use three for basic flatwork and jumping. The two more extreme positions are three-point behind the motion and the two point. The three-point behind the motion is where the rider sits very deep in the saddle, with her shoulders behind her hips with both legs wrapped firmly around her horse's sides. So, the three points are the rider's seat and two legs. This position is used as a very strong driving seat when the horse won't jump or won't go to the end of the ring. Basically, any time where the rider has to be more forceful, in addition to probably using spurs and a stick.

The two-point position is when only the rider's legs are in contact with the saddle, and there is no contact with the rider's seat in the saddle. I'd say this is a position used years ago when we rode more thoroughbreds. We needed to sit a little "chillier" and didn't need to use our seats to encourage our horses forward. It's probably used in hunter classes today on long approaches to single jumps. But my guess is that even those terrific riders do "touch" their saddles before the jumps!

The three seat positions I use more today I call the three-point position, the light two-point position, and the light three-point position. The three-point position is the rider sitting on the saddle on their two sitting bones and their two legs on the saddle as well. The rider's shoulders are above their hips and heels. Their knees are above their toes. This is usually the position people use in equitation flat classes at the canter. It might be used on a very short turn in a jumping class both in equitation and jumper classes. I see it more in jumper classes than equitation classes. Again, it's a fairly strong driving seat.

The two positions I use most of the time are the light two- and three-point positions. The light two-point is where the rider's two legs are on the saddle and their horse, their crotch is behind the pommel, and their hip angle is rotated slightly forward so they're on the front of their sitting bones. I like this position because the rider is "with" her horse's motion, yet close enough to the saddle if she needs to make an adjustment before a jump. By sinking a little deeper before the jump, her hip angle will automatically slightly open, and the distance that was going to appear a little short can be pulled off to look like a good jump because the rider allowed the horse to raise his withers and shoulders into her upper body.

I use the light three-point position on all the horses I jump, and it's a position I teach to all my students regardless of the division they show. As the horse approaches the jump, the rider is in the light two-point position, and a few strides (anywhere from one to three) before the jump, sinks down onto his or her sitting bones, although their hip angle is still with the horse's motion. As the horse leaves the ground, the thrust of his back end pushes the rider out of the saddle. Maybe I do this because I'm not very tall, and it give me a secure feeling that my horse, without any doubt, will be at my aids in front of any jump. I guess I just like the sense of security, and that's why I teach it to my students.

Q. At what level should a rider learn the three different jumping releases, and what are their purposes?

A. Actually, I have four jumping releases that I use depending on the rider's level. The short, medium, and long and out-of-hand (or automatic) release all have a particular function, and they are used according to the rider's level of development.

The beginner rider starts with a long crest release. This is taught until the rider's legs are secure enough so that she or he doesn't have to depend on their hands for support, and their legs are strong enough to maintain balance and equilibrium. A stride or two before the jump, the rider slides their hands halfway up the horse's neck, pushes down, and allows the horse to finish the jump before bringing their hands back. This allows the horse to jump without fear of being caught in the mouth while jumping.

As the rider's balance and leg support increases, she or he can learn a medium crest release, where the rider's hands, still following the crest of the horse's neck, and pressing against it, go approximately a quarter of the way up the neck.

Incorrect releases include hands floating above the neck or hands that come back towards the rider instead of moving forward along the neck.

Growing up in the "dark ages," I really never learned the crest release. We were taught the following release from the get-go. But in those days, much more attention was paid to taking lessons at home and then going to shows to see what we had learned and what still needed work! Unfortunately, today I see only the long release or a non-release (not short) in today's upper level equitation division. When these riders want to jump more technical courses or higher jumper courses, they need to understand and be able to use an out-of-hand release to be really successful. This release allows horses to be free in their necks and backs to "finish" their jump and effectively jump higher courses. Riders who have not developed an automatic release will greatly diminish their chances of having clear rounds.

The first exercise I use to develop a following release I learned from George Morris, about forty years ago! The instructor sets up a small vertical, about two feet six inches to three feet. As the rider approaches the jump, within the last stride, the instructor says either long or short (release). This release is *not* on top of the mane but rather on either side along the neck. After many jumps alternating and mixing the kind of release, the instructor says nothing. The rider will "automatically" follow the arc of the horse from takeoff to the ground. This is called either a following or automatic release, whereby the rider remains in contact with the horse on takeoff and landing. There will be a line from the horse's mouth through the rider's hand to the rider's

elbow. This allows the rider to control the horse throughout the jump. You don't see much of this today. It is very important for riding jumpers where you need control at all points of the jump. Once the rider can do this easily over a vertical, then add an oxer to the mix. Only when the rider's leg position is strong and secure should he try this kind of release. Otherwise the poor horse will get banged in the mouth.

The second exercise comes from Anne Kursinski. She teaches the following release using a "driving hand." In other words, turn your hands over on the reins so that your thumb is on top of the rein and it exits through your pinky. Look in a book for how the reins are held for horses that are being driven (carts). Approach a small vertical, again two feet six inches to three feet in your two-point (half seat) position with your hands about two feet apart. Once the horse leaves the ground, allow your body to stay with the flight of the horse's jump without touching his neck. If your leg is strong and secure, you will be able to easily stay with your horse without depending on your hands for balance. Then graduate to an oxer and higher fences.

Once you can stay with your horse from takeoff to landing without interfering, and maintaining your own balance, you will have learned a following or out-of-hand release. Just look at the example of Joe Fargis. He allows his horse to be totally free to use all his parts to negotiate the jump. He rides with beautiful examples of great technique, exceptional basics, and wonderful style.

Q. My horse goes to a fence in a beautiful light frame and jumps well. But he lands rooting, and pulls me to the end of the ring, practically yanking me out of the saddle. How do I get him to land and maintain the same light frame he has before the jump?

A. If your horse is light, balanced, jumps beautifully but lands heavily, rooting, and drags you to the end of the ring, I would first check his feet and ankles to make sure he is not uncomfortable. Before you think of it as a training issue, make sure it is not a physical problem. Especially if this is a new issue, I would have the horse checked by your vet. Remember, a horse lands with a great deal of pressure/stress on his feet and forelimbs!

If it is not physical but a training issue, there are a few exercises you can try. Put up a small jump (about two feet six inches) about two strides parallel to the ring wall or fence. Put two ground poles on the back side of the jump perpendicular from your jump to the wall so it creates a chute. Jump the small jump and stop immediately in front of the wall/fence. In a soft voice say, "whoa" and use light hands. Turn left or right and walk over the ground pole. Then again trot or canter over the small jump again. Repeat this exercise until your horse anticipates stopping.

Then pull the jump farther back from the wall/fence, maybe three or four strides. Again, repeat the exercise until your horse makes the connection of your voice, hands, and wall/fence.

If possible, keep this exercise up in your ring. Then, in time, jump other jumps in your ring, but if he starts to get strong again, go back to your "chute".

Another exercise is to put a pole on the ground four or five strides after one jump. Trot or canter over the jump and *stop* before the ground pole. If your horse tries to "pull" you over the pole, use enough hand to "make him stop". You may have to be strong at first, *but* I do not mean *rough*! Then back him up and walk over the pole. Rehearse these many times until your horse anticipates being stopped. Then canter the jump and the ground pole and stop on a straight line. If your horse pulls after the ground pole, go back and repeat the jump and stop again before the ground pole.

Horses learn by a process called conditioning. To teach a horse learned behavior, it must be repeated so many times until your specific aid results in your horse's specific response.

Q. My horse is a spooky jumper. If the jump looks scary to him, he'll practically jump the top of the standards. Is there a way to get him to settle down and jump normally? I thought he was just green, but it's been a year now and he hasn't gotten any better.

A. Actually, it's great that your horse is spooky! That can either create great jumps or a disaster!

What you want to do is use the "spook" to work for you. I'd go to the Dollar Store and buy a bunch of plastic table covers in different colors and patterns. You can also buy these plastic jump covers at several tack shops, but why spend that kind of money? Then I'd drape them over very small jumps at home. While doing your flat work, just trot and canter him over many, many little jumps.

If he jumps too high, when you land, basically ride him *very* forward (I call it "gun him") away from the jump. In other words, you must make sure he stays in front of your legs! If you keep the jumps small enough, two feet to two feet six inches, I believe you can do this almost daily. Get him desensitized to the different "weird" jumps.

When you're ready to go to a horse show, bring your table covers, maybe one or two, and put them over jumps in the schooling area. Again, get him in front of your legs and ride him off the ground, across the jump and away from the jump. You want to level him out but allow him to express himself. Again, if you do this correctly, you will be able to use his "spook" to create wonderful jumps, without fear.

Q. My horse moves well and jumps around, but he's not always even in front. He doesn't hang at all; he just isn't always square. What can I do to improve his form?

A. I would suggest two exercises: For the first, place a series of bounce jumps, set at nine to ten feet apart depending on his stride. Keep the jumps low. They only need to be two feet to two feet six inches. This will make him quicker with his front end. I would suggest three or four jumps. If you have room, follow it by another jump perhaps forty-five to forty-six feet away. This should be an easy three strides. Once he understands the exercise from the bounce jumps to the small jump, do the exercise in reverse. Start with the single jump and then continue to the bounce jumps.

The second exercise is to place a small vertical (two feet to three feet) in the middle of the ring. If your horse is lower with his left foreleg, jump the fence on the left lead and in the air smoothly turn him to the right. Then on the right lead, jump the fence and smoothly turn him left or right again. Do this exercise in reverse if his right foreleg is the "lazy" leg. This exercise will force him to be quicker with his outside leg.

Any time you can set an exercise that will teach your horse, the better. Legendary horseman Rodney Jenkins told me years ago, "jumps teach horses way better than riders can teach em". I try to follow his advice every day!

Q. I have a young horse that I am just starting over fences. He's very willing, but he doesn't have a clue what to do with all four legs! Sometimes he'll jump with his front feet and just stop in the middle with the hind feet still on the takeoff side. How can I help him figure out what to do with his feet, and what kind of gymnastics would you suggest setting up?

A. That's great that your young horse is so willing to jump! It's important that you keep up his confidence and courage. The gymnastics need to be simple yet interesting to teach him how to jump correctly.

I suggest that you set up a series of three or four bounces about nine feet apart (if you trot in rather than canter in, make it six to eight feet). Start with cross rails and guide poles. By this I mean rails that are perpendicular to both sides of the jumps, which act as a chute. It's important that your horse learns to stay straight and not evade by shifting either left or right.

You'll need someone on the ground to see that your horse's stride is comfortable with these distances. You don't want your horse to get quick or slow but rather go through the exercise easily at a nice even pace. The ground person can alter the distances to accommodate your horse. This exercise will teach your horse how to manage his legs when jumping. He will lift off with his front end, and as soon as he hits the ground, his hind legs will have to follow. Keep it simple. Encourage him to be patient, straight, and confident.

Once he masters this exercise, then put another jump about twenty-one feet from the last jump (eighteen feet if you trot in). This is a simple exercise to teach your horse how to use both ends of his body without worrying him about the rider "finding distances."

Q. My horse doesn't do clean changes, often being several strides late behind or just happily cross cantering the whole corner. He jumps great, and I would like us to be successful at shows. Could you tell me how I can teach him to land on the correct lead?

A. I have two exercises I'd use to teach your horse to land on a specific lead.

1. Put a cavalletti in the corner of the ring at a forty-five-degree angle to the wall, very close to the corner. It will force your horse to land on the lead he was on. \You will start on the right lead, and he will land on the right lead. Repeat this exercise several times.

   To land on the left lead, just start in the opposite corner and repeat. Then you can add another cavalletti before the first one, so you are basically riding a circle. Repeat this exercise several times in both directions.

   With young horses I keep this exercise up in my ring so I can rehearse this gymnastic often.

2. Make a square box out of four ground poles.

Canter in and out, going straight on the right lead and the left lead from all sides. Then canter in straight and out to a rail perpendicular to the rail you jumped. This will encourage him to stay on the same lead. If you want to teach him to land on the opposite lead, canter in on one lead and change his bend and canter out on the opposite rail perpendicular to the rail you just jumped. It's an easy way to teach a horse how to do lead changes.

Q. I have a new client who flings herself at her horse whenever they jump. How do I teach her to be quiet and let her horse do the jumping?

A. I would start off by telling this rider that when she throws herself at her horse as he leaves the ground, she makes his job much harder. It is *her* job to do the flatwork to get to the jump, and it is her horse's job to jump. Just think for a moment. How does your horse know how high and wide to jump! He has to have the time, before he jumps, to "size up" the moment. If a rider jumps up his neck and interferes with him, how can he be expected to be able to make this decision? If the rider's hip angle is closed to some degree, the thrust of the horse's back end will push her up out of the saddle. Obviously the larger the jump, the more the horse will push the rider forward out of the saddle.

I would place a rail about nine feet in front of the jump if the rider is cantering and tell her that once she is over the rail, in her two-point position to wait for her horse to jump and just think of releasing him. Let him jump … stay quiet and out of his way. He will put his rider in the center of his balance if he is not interfered with. Any ducking, shoving, or diving up his neck only makes his life *more* difficult. The quieter the rider stays on takeoff, the easier it is for the horse.

I find that when I explain to my rider the horse's responsibility and her responsibility, it seems to click. The rider's job is to get her horse to the jump, and it is the horse's job to jump.

Once the rider can remain calm over one jump, I will put up a gymnastic to help her remain calm and with her horse over a series of jumps. I might start trotting a ground rail six feet out to a cross rail, then sixteen to eighteen feet to a small vertical, and then twenty-one feet to another vertical or eventually an oxer until my rider can stay in harmony with her horse

It's important that the rider understand that all unnecessary movement off the ground only makes her horse's life more difficult. The calmer she stays, the more freedom her horse has to watch the jump and jump easily.

Q. I have a very nice, athletic horse that I do the hunters with. However, sometimes he swaps leads going down the lines. How can I correct that? I had him checked by my vet, and there seems to be no problem with him physically.

A. I have a few suggestions for you. First, if your horse does lead changes easily, never practice them!

Secondly, I'd put guide poles between the jumps. In other words, put up two jumps with a related distance. Then put poles perpendicular to the two jumps. Depending on how many strides there are, put down enough guide poles to keep your horse straight. The distance between the guide poles should be about six feet.

This will help keep your horse straight and discourage him from swapping his lead. If he does a flying change, do a *simple* change back to the lead you want. If you do another flying change, you will only confuse him!

Then take away a couple of poles until he can maintain his lead between the two jumps. If he becomes anxious, put the poles back in until he relaxes and maintains his leads. He probably does this because he's anticipating his next turn.

Be patient and positive. Take your time, and he will relax, and you'll be fine.

Q. I have a hard time keeping my horse straight. He drifts in lines when he's jumping and gets wiggly and crooked. I know it's so important for him to be straight. What can I do to get him to stay straight?

A. Most horses that wiggle, whether it be on the flat or jumping, are usually behind the rider's legs. The drifting to one side could possibly be a weakness in your horse's back end. If your horse always jumps to one side, I'd have your vet check his hocks and/or stifles to see if it's a physical problem. I always check with my vet when one of my horses displays "new" issues.

If that's not the case, again, I think your horse is not going straight because he's behind your legs. Usually riding your horse forward will take care of his wiggle and drift. I would do a lot of transitions both between gaits and within the gait. I would also do a good deal of lateral exercises, such as circles, leg yields, serpentines, and half turns. Keep him interested in his work.

Lateral exercises get your horse supple to your aids and allow you to put him between your hands and legs. Longitudinal exercises, forward and backward transitions, get your horse prompt to your hand and leg aids.

I'd put ground poles perpendicular both before and after the jumps to keep him straight. Think of creating a chute. Another good exercise would be cross rails and Swedish oxers to teach him to go straight. Find exercises that will teach your horse. Jumping exercises will teach horses more than you as a rider will teach them.

It's also extremely important to be patient and consistent with your training program. When you jump, always keep rails perpendicular both on takeoff and landing until he learns how to back up and stay straight. Then I'd take away the poles before the jump and keep the landing poles after the jump until he learns how to stay centered.

Q. My horse had been laid up for a while with an injury. Now he's back in work, and we've just started jumping again. He's a little too excited. What kind of exercises can we do to get him jumping again but still keep him under control?

A. Start out with some poles on the ground scattered around the ring. Don't think, "I'll do flatwork first, then poles." Instead, intermingle them so it's not like, "Oh, wow, now we're going to jump." Walk, trot, and canter over the poles. If he gets excited at one gait, go back to a slower one.

The good news is he's excited and wants to jump. So, his reward is to allow him to jump at whichever gait he stays quiet in. His correction is, "No, you can't do it." If he gets quick, either circle away or use a downward transition to a slower gait. Maybe just walk over the pole or go over it at a slow trot.

Next, you can move up to cavalletti or blocks. Start with the lowest height and then rotate them to move up to a higher rung, and then the highest one.

I'm not a believer in more bridle or yanking a horse up. I don't want to kill the horse's enthusiasm by punishing him when he wants to go. I want to redirect his attention to the rider.

Depending on the size of the jump, and whether you approach it at the trot or the canter, you can also place a pole on the landing side, anywhere from eight to ten feet away from the jump. Since he's so eager, put the rail a little on the closer side. Put a placement pole about nine or ten feet in front of the jump. Make sure you have a knowledgeable person on the ground to

adjust the space to fit your horse's stride. You want to create a very even stride between the jump and the pole, using the jump to train the horse.

Q. My young horse has no problem doing flying changes at home, but when we get to a show, it's different. He gets nervous and distracted, and we either miss a change completely, or end up cross cantering. What can I do?

A. The good news is that your horse does it at home, so you know that he already has learned the changes.

At a show, your horse is anxious in the new environment. The most important thing is to get him comfortable. So, don't worry about the changes yet. If you land on the wrong lead, bring your horse back to a trot. Trot until your horse takes a breath, and then ask him to pick up the new lead. Do it in a relaxed fashion, not breaking from the canter and then running into the new lead.

You can also circle. If your horse gets really tense, you can land, go back to a trot, and circle, letting your horse relax and take a breath before you resume your canter and continue your course. You can do this twice on a course just don't do it three times, or you will be eliminated!

Q. How do you teach your riders eye control going to a jump?

A. I tell them there are four things they have to think about, but they come at different times so, they don't have to consider too much information all at once.

1. Establish a canter that will give you two options, where you can invisibly change your horse's stride before the jump. In other words, I'm going to assume you ride well enough that your horse reacts to your aids. So, if you need to, you can smoothly move up the last couple of strides without having to make a big obvious move. Conversely, you can slow down or shorten your horse's stride without being obvious. So, on your opening circle, ask yourself those two questions; if you know you have two options, then your pace is probably right.

2. Set your track. This is like a railroad track, with a beginning and a destination. Find something stationary past your first jump that will be your destination, and you'll want to ride to that point. Stay out in the corner until you can see that specific point between the first two standards. This will set up your track. Make sure you keep riding your horse to the middle of the jump, at the jump, and (if advanced) over the jump and after the jump.

3. Stay on your pace and track and look at the center of the top pole (or front pole of an oxer), the jump will tell you what to do when you're one, two, or three strides away. Once you know how far away the jump will be, set your eyes back to the point after the jump where you want to go after you land. Many times, further back isn't better since so many things can happen when your too far from the jump. You'll either stay with the exact same canter, move up a little, or take back a little. There's never just *one* distance. Many distances can be fine if ridden properly and not given up.

4. Jump the fence, and as you ride out the line, make any necessary adjustments such as a lead change or set your horse's canter for the next question the course asks. Then, like an endless loop, go back to step one.

Q. My horse has a short stride, and we end up having a lot of chips. Is there some exercise I can do to try and improve his stride?

A. Put three rails on the ground and make the distance between all three ground poles the same. If you have a large enough ring, I would suggest that you set them at sixty-two feet apart. Canter your horse over these three poles. Your horse will probably do five strides. See if you can encourage him to do a very steady/short six strides. Once he can do six strides, ride the line of poles in five and five strides. Then go back and do six strides and six strides again. Keep the poles/jumps at the same distance so you can teach him how to lengthen and shorten his stride. When the ground poles become actual jumps, they will be ridden in one less stride. The five strides will become four strides, and the six strides will become five strides. Be patient, and he will learn how to become more adjustable and elastic. The continuation of the exercise is his reward. If you need to stop him from increasing his stride, that is the correction.

Again, be patient with your horse and repeat this exercise until he is reactive to your aids and relaxed. It is a wonderful exercise that doesn't require your horse to "jump" a lot of jumps, but he learns to listen to your aids.

Q. My horse likes to shorten right in front of a fence. He kind of pats the ground a few times before he jumps. How do I get him to jump from a more normal distance and stride?

A. As I mention in many of my responses, that if this is a new issue for your horse, I'd get him checked by a vet to make sure there aren't any physical problems preventing him from jumping from longer distances. Many times, if a horse is concerned about landing, he will shorten his stride and want to jump closer to the jump.

However, if that is not the problem, I would put a "takeoff pole" three to four feet in front of the jump . This should encourage him to jump farther away from the jump. The higher the jump, the further out the "takeoff pole" should be. You can also place another "landing" pole" nine feet after the jump and another ten feet away to encourage him to land and continue forward instead of falling to the ground in a heap.

But again, if this is a new development, have him checked by your vet to make sure he is physically sound. If you don't have access to a vet, put him on a few grams of Bute (an NSAID) for a few days and see if he is more willing to go forward. If he is, then you must find a vet to check him. If not, then try the exercise I've mentioned to see if that can help both you and your horse.

Q. How can I teach my horse to land on a certain lead? He is a jumper and not a great lead changer.

A. There are two ways you can approach this. There is a diagram in this book that you can look at and try. Put a small fence on an angle in each corner of the ring. If you do it properly, you can teach your horse to land either on the right or left lead. I'd start with a rail on the ground and then build it into a small jump. B. The other way is to use a slight opening rein as your horse leaves the ground and in midair ask him to land on the lead you want, just the way you'd ask him to pick up his lead.

When you use the opening rein, your inside hand is going away from your horse's neck… down and out a little bit. It's important that your opening rein doesn't pull back, or you're going to teach him to hollow his back in midair! The rider doesn't interfer with her horse's jump, but her head and eyes are looking into the direction she wants to go. You use your other hand as either an out of hand (following) release if you're advanced. A more intermediate rider should use a medium crest release. But your eyes and slight opening rein should encourage him to land on the lead you want .

Q. I have a young horse that is now jumping two feet six inches. He'll jump about every fourth fence spectacularly tight and round, and then be kind of casual about the others. I'm not sure if it's just too low for him at this point to think he needs to put a lot of effort into, or if I need to do something to encourage him to jump better.
What exercises or gymnastics would you recommend bringing out that beautiful jump more consistently? With his amazing rhythm, if I get him to jump well consistently, I'll have a real star on my hands!

A. These are important questions. If he's quite young, his attention span will be quite short. Young, green horses, in my opinion, will stay focused for only about twenty minutes. So, if your jumping session goes on much longer, he may be bored, and you'll lose his attention. However, if he's been jumping two feet six inches for a long time, he might be getting bored and casual. In any event, I'll give you a few suggestions to improve his consistency. If he's quite young, I'd try to shorten his training period and keep the jumps small. You could add some "interesting" jumps to keep him interested and alert without challenging him with higher jumps. Perhaps put a little tarp over the jump or put a towel or little tarp under the jump. Put up a little roll top, little wall, or an arch wall. In other words, a variety of small, but interesting jumps, not to scare him, but to pique his interest. This way you can challenge him without over facing him with higher and wider jumps.

However, if he's not so green, and is just bored, then some gymnastics could be the answer. I like a gymnastic of X's. This will keep him straight and very correct with his jump. Sometimes I'll trot over a ground pole, then eight feet to an X, then add another X at maybe eighteen feet, and another X (could be an oxer with the X in front and a straight pole behind), followed by one more X at twenty-one feet. This should encourage him to be very correct. You can "play" with the heights and distances. Then return to your normal routine. If he becomes casual, "remind" him to stay focused and correct with this exercise.

CHAPTER 3

HORSE SHOWS

Q. We asked Kip Rosenthal the same Roving Reporter question that was asked of other top professionals in the industry: "What changes would you like to see take place in the horse world?"

A. One of the things Kip would like to see take place is the elimination of the mileage rule. If you don't know or you don't understand, you can look it up in the USEF rule book. If you'd like good horse shows that care about the animal (with good footing, stabling, etc.) attract the clients, then you'll find managers that care about those issues. Right now, there are shows that continue to be run and are not horse friendly, because they are not challenged—they have the dates and know that people must come to them if they want to show, so they often don't put much effort into improving their shows.

Shows should be subject to competition, and not protected. That way the one that does the best job will be the show that draws the most exhibitors. Horses and exhibitors would benefit.

There are many venues that would love to hold shows and, would hold shows that are more in the horse's best interest; yet they are prevented from doing so because of the mileage rule. This rule often prevents those with newer, better visions from coming to the forefront.

Kip also does not like the fact that many horses now show twelve months a year, without a break, with resulting unsoundness and maintenance issues. As a professional, she says she has to become the horse's advocate. The changes in the show season and demands of showing have not been to the horse's benefit. Perhaps new qualifying criteria could be developed so that horses are not forced to show week after week.

A third issue Kip noted is the incredible division that has arisen between those who show on a local level and those who show on a national level. While those who do well on a national level generally receive nice awards and recognition, she feels that state and regional finals need to be made more special, with more recognition for those who view these finals as their year-end goals. Kip acknowledges what great events the Connecticut Hunter Jumper Association Finals and New England Finals are and encourages other groups to try to make their finals just as special.

Q. I have some students who ride very nicely at their respective level. But when they see other riders at the barn, who are more advanced, it seems to shake their own confidence. How can I get them to understand that those riders are further along in their education and training, and in time, they will also achieve that level?

A. Explain to them, that those riders achieved that level, because they've worked very hard. Riding is not an easy sport. Perhaps, you can tell them as they work towards their goal, to think of it as a journey. I've told kids to keep a journal of their lessons, as well as, their horse shows. Every month you suggest they look through their journal and highlight the things that they need to improve. If they see the same issue come up each week, month by month, maybe they need to take some responsibility to make better habits for themselves when they're riding without lessons on those days of the week. However, you need to stay positive in your approach, then your student will feel your confidence and will rise to the occasion!

Q. As a trainer and a judge, what would you say are the biggest weaknesses in equitation riders today? What should they do to improve?

A. My pet peeves in judging equitation are twofold. One is when a rider is stiff. I hate stiffness. This is evident when it looks as though the rider went through the dry cleaners and came out starched! The horse feels this tension and jumps accordingly rigid and stiff. Usually these riders' basics are good, but they're over schooled in their position so it is no longer natural but looks forced and rigid.

The other thing I dislike is the "equitation" pelham bit in the wrong hands. I hate to see a horse jammed up and his poll behind a vertical line to the ground. Years ago, we learned how to use the pelham … how the two reins worked. Today so many equitation horses are bitted in pelhams and their riders just hold both reins with no idea how this bit works, especially on the flat. I hate to see a horse riding behind the bit with his nose tucked into his chest. Unfortunately, I see this all too often.

Many equitation horses show in various kinds of pelhams today. It's a wonderful bit when used correctly, but in my eyes, I see it abused by riders with uneducated hands, so their horses are forced just to deal with it. It's nice to see that advanced riders understand how the pelham bit affects their horses and they use the bit correctly.

Q. I would like to do both hunters and the big eq, but my family doesn't have the money for a string of horses. I know years ago people did both with one horse. Is that still doable, and if so, how should I go about it?

A. Years ago, we used our junior hunters or junior jumpers to double up as our equitation horses. I had a horse named Rome Dome and was reserve champion in the AHSA (now USEF) Medal finals at Harrisburg. That next week at Harrisburg, in the same ring, I won the Grand Prix on the same horse!

Unfortunately, as our sport has evolved, equitation horses have become specialists. They must have the smoothness, big scopey stride, attractiveness, and rideability of our hunters. They also have to have the bravery, carefulness, elastic stride, and the ability to answer all the formulas that courses ask today that one would find in the jumper divisions.

As I'm sure you know, most of our horses come from Europe, where there are no equitation or hunter classes, so all these horses probably have had some experience in the jumper division, depending on the horse's age. Therefore, I suggest you look for a horse that might be able to do both the divisions you want to compete in. You might have to prioritize which division is more important to you: perhaps a horse that will be a very good equitation horse and a possible ribbon in the hunters, or a horse more suitable for the hunters but only passable in equitation.

Once qualified for whatever equitation finals you want to do, maybe you could look into leasing a horse for that weekend that might give you a better shot at a ribbon. That way you can use one horse to qualify for both hunters and equitation and spend a little more for a lease. This certainly will cost much less than having two horses for a year or even many years.

So yes, I do think it's possible, but you'll have to look around and have a good idea what you really want and what you will settle for. Good luck in your pursuit! He or she is out there!

Q. My horse is a little stiff, crooked and mainly late to my hands and legs. How do I make him better so I can be more competitive in equitation classes, which I love?

A. Your horse needs to "always be" at your aids, immediately but relaxed. Lots of transitions, both within the gait and between gaits, will make your horse prompt to going forward and coming back. Lateral exercises, such as circles, half turns, half turns in reverse, serpentine, and broken lines, will help supple your horse. When horses are stiff, they are crooked. All the lateral exercises I've mentioned will help supple your horse. When horses are supple, they will ride straight.

It's so important for you to have a program that's consistent. Your aids are how you communicate with your horse. The exercises I've mentioned should help you teach your horse to become well educated to perform all the tests that can be asked for in the hunter seat equitation division.

Q. It looks like my horse and I will be going to indoors, both Harrisburg and Washington, for the first time! I'm very excited, but also nervous. How do I prepare my horse for being inside with all that activity?

A. Yes, going "indoors" for the first time can be very intimidating! I offer you two suggestions. One, take your horse, if possible, to a few local indoor facilities, where you can pay to school your horse in a new environment. Try and jump a few jumps, in a schooling area, if possible, to prepare and get him ready, as you would do at any show. Then enter the "new" arena and jump a course at the height you will be showing. See how both you and he acclimate to the new setting. This will give you information for how you'll need to prepare him for indoors. You might try and do this a few times.

Second, remember your horse will most likely feel your composure or your nerves. When showing in the hunters' or the equitation divisions, you are dealing with subjective results. The only thing you can control is how you ride your horse. So, the best advice I can give you is for you to ride your horse to the best of your ability so he can feel comfortable and perform the best he can for you. That is all you can control, whatever happens in subjective classes, the judging is outside of your control. But you owe your horse your confidence, focus, and the ride he is used to.

Q. I have a really nice four-year-old that I want to keep sound and competitive for as long as possible. I see too many horses being pushed too hard too fast and disappearing from the show ring at a young age. How should I handle his career to best keep him sound?

A. This is an interesting question for there are no "absolute" answers. I'm sure different professionals will have many different answers from their own experiences. For me, however, there are a few important questions you need to ask yourself.

How mature is his physical, mental, and emotional development? Most horses have not fully grown at four years. Is he still getting taller or just filling out?

Remember, horses were not put on this earth to be ridden over jumps. They are front weight bearing animals. Their bodies need to be fairly developed to handle the stress jumps put on both their front and back ends.

How does he handle new situations? Is he relaxed and confident in himself? How far along is his schooling? Does he do flying changes yet? How high has he been jumping? What will it take to prepare him to show? Will you need to lunge him or ride him an hour or so before the first class? What are your long- term and short-term goals other than keeping him as sound as possible? Do you have a trainer or ground person to help you?

Only you, and your trainer if you have one, can answer these questions.

I always err on the side of being conservative. If you have a car or truck and trailer, I would take him to some shows and just school him or just ride him around the grounds and see how he copes being away from his own barn and ring. This will give you information about his attitude and self-confidence. If and when he is relaxed in the new environment, I would go to a show that had a ticketed warm-up or a schooling show (not USEF). I would start at an unrecognized show since the fees will be lower. You will not have USEF fees, or office fees, and usually, the entry fees are lower. Maybe go in some under saddle classes to see how he adjusts to other horses in a new ring. All of this will give you information that you'll need to know when he's ready to show.

Q. I want to set a major goal for my horse and myself this year. I'd like to work to win a zone or national award. But I don't want to do it at the expense of my horse. How can I balance attaining my goal without pushing my horse too much?

A. This question poses other questions that you need to think about in order to understand what your goals for the year will be. There is a big difference between zone and national awards. When you are competing for zone awards, only points/money won in your zone will count toward those awards. However, national awards are won by amassing the most points/money throughout the United States.

Depending on your zone and your division, it can be very easy to be zone champion or very difficult. You should find out how many points (in hunters) or money (in jumpers) it took to win in 2019, or the preceding year. That will give you an idea of how much you will need to win and show.

Some divisions are much more competitive than others, such as children's hunters and jumpers, children's ponies, and adult hunters and jumpers. Since these divisions are rated "C," not AA, A, or B, it might take a lot of showing to amass enough points or money to be in the upper end of your division. In the junior and amateur hunter and jumper divisions, it may take much less. You will have to do your homework to see if these goals are attainable. To win national year-end awards in the hunter and jumper divisions, you will have to compete at the highest competition level and have a *great* horse or a very fast trailer or van!

There are now excellent unrecognized shows in many areas (zones) throughout the country. These shows are less expensive because you don't have all the USET and USEF dues and other expenses. Many are held in beautiful venues with excellent rings, jumps, footing, and

judges, as well as all the other benefits you'd see at our top-rated shows. Many even offer circuit awards. This might be something to look for in your area.

Q. I just got my first really fancy hunter, and now I want to pursue my lifelong dream of qualifying for indoors in the amateur-owner division. What do I need to know about qualifying for, and competing in, the indoor circuit?

A. Good luck in pursuing your lifelong dream! Qualifying for the indoor shows depends on many variables. You should find out how many points were necessary in the past two years to know what you will probably need to be accepted. You can contact the shows you are interested in attending to gain this information, although points from year to year tend to be pretty much the same. Once you find out this information, you and your trainer should get together to "map out" a show schedule to best maximize your time, finances, and horse management. Shows that offer AA divisions will render more points than A shows. Also, the number of horses showing in your division will determine the point values.

You should first look into shows in your area to find out the show rating and the number of people in your division. Your trainer should know this information. You can then plan a show schedule from the dates when the new qualifying season begins until it ends. The three indoor shows: Harrisburg, Washington, and the National—all have different qualifying dates.

Q. My eight year old gelding plays on the turns. He jumps great, has easy lead changes, is brave and honest, but he just loves to play and give little bucks on the turns. This behavior keeps us from getting good ribbons at the horse shows. He does this at home, too, but not as much as at the horse shows. What can I do?

A. That's great that he feels so good about himself! However, in the hunter/equitation ring, such exuberance is frowned upon. Since he does this at home, it makes it pretty easy to eliminate this behavior. When you are schooling him at home and he "plays" on the turns, you can do one of two things to eliminate his friskiness. If he is jubilant, make him trot on a circle and don't canter and approach the next jump until he is respectful and obedient to your aids.

Remember how horses learn: a process called conditioning. He obviously enjoys jumping, so his reward is to continue on course, and his correction is to circle until he behaves himself. You must be consistent with this program even if you need to circle him in the show ring until he pays attention. If he really wants to continue jumping, this correction is the best method. He must be obedient, or he will not be allowed to continue jumping.

If his "playfulness" is more extreme, then halt him when he becomes too exuberant. Then make him circle until his behavior improves. The main thing is to eliminate this behavior at home and be willing to do the same at the horse show. I think once he's better mannered at home, he will be better in the show ring. If not, do the same in the ring. Don't correct him with your own emotion. Be very professional and very consistent in your approach to his problem. It should be easy to correct this behavior if you're willing to be consistent. That is the key!

Q. My pony is really good in the jumping classes, but he fusses with his head/bit in the under saddle classes. He is a good mover, but we never get a ribbon. What should I do?

A. Even though your pony is good over fences, since you have a problem with him in the under saddle classes, make sure you have a good equine dentist check your pony's teeth and bite two times a year. The dentist can also tell you if your pony has a "shallow" mouth. This means that the roof of your pony's mouth doesn't have a lot of room to handle a bit that is jointed. If you have already done that, then try a couple of different kinds of bits. He might be more comfortable with a straight rubber snaffle, a "happy mouth," or a Mylar bit. You just need to try a few different bits to find out what is most comfortable for your pony.

Lastly, make sure that you keep the bit in the corners of your pony's mouth. That means a straight line from his or her mouth through your wrists to your elbows. If you are pulling down on your pony's mouth so that you are riding on his bars (a very sensitive area where there are no teeth), then your pony could be objecting to the pressure that you are putting on this sensitive area.

Q. I show in the junior hunters, and I hear that hunter judges are being encouraged to let horses show their enthusiasm and expression more than before. I'm not sure what this means. Could you explain it to me and let me know what it means to me as the rider?

A. I'm not sure what that means either. My guess is that since the distances between the jumps don't allow a real "scopey" horse to show off, you could show a gallop to single jumps on the course.

Also, today all the rated hunters, such as the junior, amateur, and performance divisions, have brought back the handy hunter classes. That is a great way to "show off" your horse. Judges are encouraged to reward horses that answer the posed questions with shorter turns and show more brilliance to individual fences. For instance, gallop directly to the first jump from the in gate and pull up smoothly after the last jump and walk directly to the out gate instead of opening and closing circles.

These are great classes that were the norm years ago and, thankfully, have been brought back today. It's definitely a way to show your horse's enthusiasm, expression, and brilliance. Other classes that have become extremely popular are the Hunter Derbies. Those classes are offered at different heights and some of the Derbies now offer a large amount of prize money.

Q. I've always leased before, but I finally bought my first horse. He's ten years old and is a good guy with lots of experience. I see something very often at shows that I want to avoid. So many horses go in what I think are way too many classes. At one show I was at, one horse did twenty-four classes in three days—and I'm not talking cross rails! How can I figure out how much is okay for my horse to do without overtaxing him and risking his future?

A. This is a good question. Horses have only so many quality jumps in them. The higher the jumps, the less you want to tax your horse. I think that low fences, let's say two feet to two feet six inches, are pretty easy on the average sound horse, so your horse can jump more fences at that level. At three feet, I usually keep my horses, when showing, to three or four courses in one day. When the jumps get to three feet six inches, I try to keep my horses to three classes in one day. It will depend on how much you need to get your horse prepared.

Do you need to lunge or ride your horse before the show? Lunging is very taxing on your horse. I prefer in the morning a twenty-minute ride to relax my horses and get them attentive to my aids. Almost all my clients have only one horse, so that horse has to be used to teach its rider lessons and to gain experience. That same horse also has to be competitive at the important and very high level A horse shows. Horses have only so many quality jumps in them. So, I *stress* flatwork. Think of a jumping round. How much time is "spent in the air", and how much time is the rider cantering between the jumps? The *most* important part of jumping is your flatwork!

Another question you need to ask yourself is do you need to medicate your horse with a NSAID to perform? Only one NSAID is acceptable but several are approved. If you're unsure, check with your vet or contact the USEF Drugs and Medication Department and they can answer any questions about acceptable medications, dosage amounts and hours away from competition that you can medicate your horse. How much medication does it take for your horse to be comfortable to compete?

Your horse will dictate how much he can do, if you're willing to listen.

Q. I will be heading off to college in the fall, and I look forward to riding in intercollegiate competitions. What can I expect, and what would be the best way to prepare?

A. The nice thing about intercollegiate competitions for those who haven't done a lot of showing before is it gives the opportunity to them to do what they haven't been able to do before (and at a much lower cost). For people who have had a lot of show experience, intercollegiate gives them a chance to be a part of a team and enjoy the camaraderie that goes along with that. It's very different from what "normal" show riders are used to.

One of the advantages of intercollegiate competition is that there are all levels, from beginners (walk/ trot) to open classes. And no matter what division you ride in, you can aspire to compete in Regionals and even the Intercollegiate Horse Shows Association National Championships.

In intercollegiate shows, riders draw horses' names out of a hat to determine which one they will ride. (No one competes on their own horse.) Horses are either owned by the college, or borrowed from other colleges, and riders go in cold, with no chance to warm up. Riders cannot use their own tack; they must use what the horses are wearing. Crops or spurs can only be used if they are permitted on the particular horse.

Horses are chosen for the class according to their suitability: for instance, a hot horse would not be used in a lower level class. However, for the most part, these horses are not what a person used to showing would be familiar with riding. They are donations to the college program and they are donated for a reason. It may be a soundness issue (the horse won't pass the vet), a medical issue (something that cannot be controlled with specific drugs or care), or a behavioral issue (the horse might have a spook or lead problems).

This can prove an actual advantage to riders who have never owned their own horse or showed but have been riding school horses and borrowed mounts. These riders often shine at intercollegiate shows, where they may not be the prettiest rider, but can get on and get the job done!

My advice to prepare is to ride as many horses, or as many different types, as you possibly can. And keep in mind that in intercollegiate shows, you may be riding in some very good company, not only among those who have shown already, but among those who come in unknown and become stars intercollegiate and beyond. The winner one year at the National Championships in the Open Division was Greg Best, who went on to become an Olympic medal winner.

Q. I've heard there is a growing concern in about the way horses are treated to make them quiet for hunter and equitation classes, especially during the indoor horse show season. What is your suggestion to eliminate the over lunging, over riding, all night on the treadmill, withdrawing water, tying the horse(s) up all night, numerous tubes of Perfect Prep and medications that can't be detected, and so on?

A. I wish I had the answer to this question. I know many committees are working on this very question to try and come up with solutions. It's not being swept under the carpet. Earnest Oare, a very respected horseman, wrote a letter to the *Chronicle of the Horse* stating his solution, in which he suggested a small dose of a tranquilizer, would be kinder to the horse . I also wrote a letter to the *Chronicle* as a satirical piece saying what the horses talk about when the "lights go out" during the night. They, too, would like to be lightly tranquilized rather than all the things you stated. This suggestion will never happen. The USEF and the USHJA couldn't endorse this suggestion, even if they wanted to, which they *don't*. They are following the FEI guidelines in this matter, which is very anti medication for all athletes', including horses!

I think one thing they could do at Harrisburg, where the USEF Medal Finals are held, would be to lock the lights off in the schooling areas at midnight until 5:00 a.m. the morning of the Finals. This would end the all-night riding. The show could have one of their stewards walk through the barn areas throughout the night to ensure horses weren't tied up all night and the horses had water buckets in their stalls. But there are grassy areas outside the building where horses are lunged, and that probably couldn't be monitored. I don't think the Perfect Prep issue could be monitored either nor could many injectable medications, unless we go with FEI rules, which I'm sure we don't want either.

I don't think we're going to change the way equitation nor hunter classes are judged. Minor mistakes are still going to count against the rider/horse in these classes and will probably eliminate them from placing. The different committees have their work cut out for them to find solutions to these problems before groups like PETA visit our venues!

Maybe it's time for professionals to be honest and authentic with their clients, parents, and children, and tell them this is a "sport" and we're dealing with animals, not golf clubs nor tennis rackets. Sometimes our "animals" make mistakes, and we have to understand they don't realize this is an important event! They are not inanimate objects, and although it's tremendously disappointing, life does go on. It's the highs and lows of the sport.

Q. I'm showing in the equitation, working my way up the ranks. Could you explain to me a little about what you, as a judge, look for when you are watching an equitation round or flat class?

A. Okay let's start with a flat class. In the equitation section of the rule book, it says, "You're being judged from the moment you enter the ring until the moment you leave." *But* understand, in truth, once you enter the ring for a flat class, most judges start writing numbers down on their card and get a pretty good feel for the class before it even starts. So, I always tell my riders and people I teach in clinics to enter the ring doing what you do best! In other words, do not enter the ring at a sitting trot unless you can sit the trot like Robert Dover (one of our international Olympic dressage riders)! Sitting trot can be very difficult if your horse is bouncy, so don't do it unless asked. In an advanced open eq class, you might enter the ring on a correct counter canter or a lengthening posting/rising trot—anything you can do to "show off" to attract the judge's eye. But don't do anything where you don't excel.

The Judge

Before you enter the ring, know where the judge is sitting or standing. If the judge is on the outside of the ring, make sure when you are riding across the ring, you're on the inside track, and when near the judge you're on the outside track. In other words, keep your back number obvious, easy to see and read. Remember, it's not the judge's job to find you. It's your job to be seen. If, however, the judge is in the middle of the ring (not if I'm judging!), get a "feel" for where the judge is watching, so if you need to give your horse a strong half halt, you can do that to "set up" your horse before the judge sees you. I know only a few people who still judge from the middle of the ring! You should know who they are.

First Impressions

In equitation flat classes you need to understand that you're an actor or actress onstage. When I judge a flat class, I first get a sense of the "whole" picture or the horse and rider's position and balance. Then I start by watching the position of the rider's foot in the stirrup … leg position … base of support … upper body position … the rider's hand to horse's mouth connection, and so on.

In other words, similar to a building, the position starts in the basement from the foot and goes to the rider's head. If the strength in the lower leg is incorrect, the "building" will not be secure.

Jumping Classes

In a jumping class, the rider *is* being judged from the moment he or she enters the ring until he or she leaves. This means both the opening and closing circle tells me a lot about the rider. All equitation classes are courses made up of a series of formulas, from very simple to the complex. All these formulas should be practiced at home in your riding lessons. Nothing should come as a surprise! A simple course can be a short stirrup class where the course is twice around. Even beginner riders should be taught that the second time around, their ponies or horses will probably get stronger. In my mind, the strides and canter should stay the same, not leave strides out the second time around.

In more advanced classes, I want to see that the rider understands the questions that are being asked and they ride their horse to the best of their ability so that the horse jumps the best he can.

The rhythm, balance, and canters stay the same. The canter doesn't change for the jumps. The rider should stay in the center of the horse… not ahead nor behind the motion. The rider and horse act as one. The rider's aids are invisible. Anything obvious is noted and probably wrong, or, at best, late

In my mind, rails down are very subjective. With some judges in equitation classes it's an automatic sixty-five score. Other judges take four points off the score. Obviously, in most hunter classes horses will not place with a rail down, nor will they in most jumper classes. However, in equitation classes, if a rail falls, I look to see if the rider created the four faults. If it's a poor jump, then the jump is marked as bad and will probably not place in the ribbons, depending on the level of the class. However, if the horse slightly rubs the rail and it comes down in an otherwise great ride, I would allow that rider to win over another rider whose round wasn't as good without a rail down. Again, in equitation classes it's a very subjective call.

Today riders are so schooled riding the various formulas that it's fun to watch. Equitation used to use horses not good enough to be great hunters or jumpers. Now today's elite equitation horses must have the qualities of both the hunters and jumpers. They must have an uphill carriage, be attractive, have a great canter step, be brave, have very adjustable strides, and have great natural balance, and be almost robotic in nature. The great equitation horses today are usually hard to find and very expensive. But if you have time and patience, you can find an uphill green horse with a great canter, and you can make him into a wonderful equitation horse.

Q. I would like to do both hunters and the big eq, but my family doesn't have the money for a string of horses. I know years ago people did both with one horse. Is that still doable, and if so, how should I go about it?

A. Years ago, we used our junior hunters or junior jumpers to double up as our equitation horses. I had a horse named Rome Dome and was reserve champion in the AHSA (now USEF) Medal finals at Harrisburg. That next week at Harrisburg, I won the Grand Prix on the same horse.

Unfortunately, as our sport has evolved, equitation horses have become specialists. They must have the smoothness, big scopey stride, attractiveness, and rideability of our hunters. They also have to have the bravery, carefulness, elastic stride, and the ability to answer all the formulas that courses ask for today that one would find in the jumper divisions.

As I'm sure you know, many of our horses come from Europe, where there are no ***Qequitation or hunter classes, so all these horses probably have some experience in the jumper division, depending on the horse's age. Therefore, I suggest you look for a horse that might be able to do both the divisions you want to compete in. You might have to prioritize which division is more important to you: perhaps a horse that will be a very good equitation horse and a "ribbon winner" in the hunters, or a horse more suitable for the hunters and but only passable in the equitation.

Once qualified for whatever equitation finals you want to do, maybe you could look into leasing a horse for that weekend that might give you a better shot at a ribbon. That way you can use one horse to qualify for both hunters and equitation and spend a little more for a lease. This certainly will cost much less than having two horses for a year or even many years.

So yes, I do think it's possible, but you'll have to look around and have a good idea what you really want and what you will settle for. Good luck in your pursuit! He or she is out there!

Q. My horse loves to jump and is always so well behaved except when he is in company with other horses in under saddle classes. He hates having other horses close to him, and we have lost many a ribbon in the under saddle classes because of it. I try to take as many group lessons as possible to get him used to being with other horses, but he still acts up at the horse shows. What can I do?

A. This is a tough one. I had a wonderful junior hunter named Arrivaderci who won many, many classes over fences. He would hack fine in the first direction, then become very strong and tense in the second direction. There are a lot of horses who just don't hack well, even if they could be the under saddle winner.

I think you have two choices. One, go to some unrecognized shows, tranquilize him, and show him in a bunch of flat classes. Maybe by allowing him to relax with some medication, he will find these classes aren't so terrible. Then, after enough "calm" experiences, see if he will stay relaxed at these shows with no medication.

Then try him again at recognized shows, obviously with no medication, and see if he can stay relaxed. If he does, great!

If not, you might just have to depend on his classes over jumps to win enough to be champion or reserve. I wish I had a better answer for you, but some horses just won't hack even if they are normally quiet horses. A great many champion hunters are just not happy and relaxed in under saddle classes.

Q. I know a number of people who use non-conventional stirrups due to joint issues and who want to show in equitation classes. Could you please explain the rule about stirrups in equitation classes, it's purpose, and how a rider needing non-conventional stirrups could use them?

A. It was a rule that black stirrups could not be used in equitation classes. That has been changed to a judge *may* penalize riders who use black stirrups in equitation classes. The easy answer is that if you are riding, with black boots, on a dark-colored horse in equitation classes and I can't distinguish your leg from your horse, I really can't judge whether your leg position is correct or not. It's possible that a rider could *lose* a stirrup for several steps, and I would not see it. That rider could end up winning an equitation class, but if the rider had used a stirrup I could see, that would have been considered a major fault. How would you like to be beaten by this rider?

I don't mind the silver stirrup that has the small elastic black band on the stirrup branch that reduces stress on the ankle and knee joints. There are also very light silver stirrups and silver safety stirrups that are acceptable in equitation classes. I just need to see the rider's leg position to "judge them". However, being a traditionalist, neither do I want to see the "new" colored stirrups in the equitation division. By colored I mean the red, pink, blue green, and so on. I'm from the "old school". I want the equitation division to remain classical. Use those colorful stirrups in the jumper division. There are many stirrups on the market today that are more comfortable for people with joint problems, and many are silver. I'm sure if you look, you'll find them.

Q. What dressage movements would my horse need to know for testing in the open equitation classes? And could you give a brief description of each movement?

A. This is an interesting question. I suggest you go to the USEF.org website and look up two specific divisions. The first is the equitation section, (EQ113). This will give you the information on all the tests from which the judges must choose. You will see that by age and/or class level (maiden, novice, limit, intermediate, open), the different tests can be used.

Once you find out the different tests that judges can ask for, then go to the dressage section to find out how to perform these movements. Go to (DR101), Object and Principles of Dressage. In this section you will see halt and/or back (DR 102/106). This is the first test in

When you look in the Rule Book in the Hunter Seat Equitation section, it will also tell you about figure eights at the trot and canter (DR110c). These are tests three and four in hunter seat equitation.

Our test number five, work collectively at the walk, trot, and canter, is (DR103-105). Execute a serpentine at the trot and canter is (DR110b). These specific test sections will help you understand how the different tests should be performed.

Now it's necessary to find out how to supple your horse to be elastic, and straight and work with impulsion. Go to (DR111) to understand suppling, shoulder-in, and leg yield. Collection can be found in (DR115). Impulsion will be (DR116).

CHAPTER FOUR

PSYCHOLOGY ISSUES

Q. I'm too concerned about pleasing my parents and my teacher that I don't think about riding my horse when I'm in an equitation class at a horse show. Then if I make a mistake, my round just spirals down from there. How can I have more confidence in myself and stay focused when I'm in the ring?

A. Well, the first thing you need to think about is pleasing (riding) your horse so he knows what you want him to do and when you want him to do it … to listen to your aids. Otherwise he's going to wonder what's going on. Basically, the only thing you can control is your horse to the best of your ability at that moment in time. You can't control the judge, and you can't control what other people think and feel. If you have trouble staying focused, I have a great exercise that will help put you in the "zone".

You probably have a phone that has a stopwatch and a computer with graphic designs. Take both those instruments to your bedroom or a quiet place where there will be absolutely *no* disturbances … no phone, radio, TV, or people talking. Put a graphic design on your computer, something that constantly moves. Then set your timer to run for ten seconds, then increase the time to twenty seconds, then thirty seconds … all the way to one hundred twenty seconds in increments of ten seconds each time to one hundred and twenty seconds (two minutes). Keep watching the computer screen. That's usually the time you're in the ring. If your mind wanders and you lose your concentration, reset the timer to ten seconds and start again. It will take you several trials to accomplish one hundred and twenty seconds! Make sure you're able to stay focused for two minutes pretty easily, without losing your concentration. Then take your computer and phone to a busy area where people are talking, the phone might ring, or people are going in and out of the room. Then again, put your computer and stopwatch on a table, and do the same exercise. The goal is for you to stay focused on the computer screen for one hundred twenty seconds. Again, if you lose your concentration, reset the timer to ten seconds and start again. Once you're able to do this, you'll teach yourself to get into the "zone" and stay focused when you go into the show ring. You'll be able to communicate with your horse and eliminate any distractions from your mind and stay totally on the job of riding your horse.

Q. I have a lovely eight year old student who's very happy in the barn when she's brushing and playing with the school ponies, but when it's time for her to ride, she "freezes up", and it takes me twenty minutes to finally get her on. However, once she's on, she's fine and has a great time. What would you suggest I do so it doesn't take me so long to get her on? It's very draining on me and makes the other kids just hang around until she finally gets on.

A. Well, a few things come… to my mind. First of all, since she's only eight years old, perhaps she's not ready to ride or, possibly, ride in a group. It's interesting that once she's on, she's fine and has fun. For starters, I'd probably work with her privately for a while even if she has to ride for less time due to finances, since a private lesson is normally more expensive than a group lesson. I'd explain to her mother, father, nanny, or whoever brings her to the barn what's going on. Perhaps since she enjoys being in the barn, let her "hang" out with the other kids but ride separately for a little while. I'd also ask her what she like best when she rides.

See if you can get her to play games. I once taught a child who was fearful, so I'd have her make continuous circles around me as I moved around the ring. I'd dart all around, and she'd have to chase me at the trot … I'd sleep pretty well that night! Then I'd get her to canter circles around me, but I'd have her stay on one lead and after a while change directions. Another game would be to put her on the lunge line and count out loud. Usually I have my riders count by five to one hundred and then back to zero from one hundred by fives and, then by twos. That may be too advanced for a second or third grader, but you could have her count from one to one hundred within the pony's stride or even one to twenty and see if she can count from twenty back to one. This does several things. One, counting out loud within the pony's stride will make her breathe so her body will relax before she passes out! Secondly, it will take her mind off riding, and she'll have to think what number comes next, especially when counting backwards. These are just two games that I've used, but there are many, many more. You just need to be a little creative.

One of my all-time best junior riders started out this way. A little fearful… but the games helped her relax and have fun. As she grew older and became quite serious, she became "light's out"! Ice-cold water ran through her veins! She learned how to conquer her fear and became extremely successful in the jumper division!

Q, I qualified for the Finals for the indoor shows this fall. I'm so excited and it will be the first time for both me and my horse. Do you have any suggestions I can use to help get myself and my horse ready for these shows?

A. Yes, going "indoors" for the first time can be very intimidating! I offer you two suggestions. One, take your horse, if possible, to a few local indoor facilities where you can pay to school your horse in a new environment. Try and jump a few jumps to prepare and get him ready, as you would do at any show, and then enter the "new" arena and jump a course at the height you will be showing. See how both you and he acclimate to the new setting. This will give you information for how you'll need to prepare him for indoors. You might try and do this a few times.

Second, remember your horse will most likely feel your composure or your nerves. When showing in the hunters or the equitation divisions, you are dealing with subjective results. The only thing you can control is how you ride your horse. So, the best advice I can give you is for you to ride your horse to the best of your ability so he can feel comfortable and perform the best he can for you. That is all you can control. Whatever happens with the judging it is outside your control. But you owe your horse your confidence, focus, and the ride he is used to.

Q. I took my daughter out of the barn where she was riding because the trainer there was not supportive. In fact, she could be pretty negative. My daughter shows a lot of potential, and I want to be sure to get her in a barn with a supportive trainer who will help her realize that potential. Could you give me an idea as to how I could go about finding the right fit?

A. I have a few suggestions that might be helpful in finding a more supportive trainer to teach your daughter.

First, does she have friends who ride at other barns in your area? That could be very helpful. If so, perhaps she could "visit" them at their barns and watch some lessons. She'll probably get the best "feel" that way. Obviously, if she could have a riding lesson, that would be best, but that's not always possible.

Another thing you and she can do is go to a horse show, and stand by the schooling rings, and watch how trainers interact with their students. Then go to the show ring and stand by unobtrusively, and again get a sense of how the pro talks to his or her students both before going into the ring and when the riders exit This should give you an idea of whether you like the interaction between the trainer and student.

Finally, set up a meeting with the potential trainer and discuss your daughter's goals and see if it looks like a good match. Also look at the facility. Does the staff seem competent? Are the stalls clean, and do they have good ventilation? What are the riding rings like? Is there turnout? Are there safety systems? Ask about any other concerns you will have for your horse's protection and safety.

Q. I want to qualify for the Medal/Maclay/USET finals. I have a good horse and a good trainer, but I get nervous at horse shows. My trainer says I put too much pressure on myself, and then I blow it. What should I do?

A. First, remember that there is only one thing you have control over when you are riding in a subjective division such as equitation and hunters, and that is the ride that you give your horse. You owe your horse the best ride that you can give him. You can't control how the class is being judged, but you can control how you ride.

You may not realize that the qualification rules have been changed. You no longer need to win the Maclay class in order for it to count. Now, as in the USEF Medal, the top four places count for points towards qualifying. The USEF Equitation Committee felt that the stress of having to win was too much, with kids having great rounds and then being disappointed with a second place. Without the pressure of knowing that you have to win, it should be easier to relax, put in a good round, and get a good ribbon. The new system is designed to reduce pressure and should help prevent wear and tear on horses and riders, who sometimes ran to two different shows in one day in order to try to achieve a first-place win.

Another change to keep in mind is that you can now continue to show after you have qualified. This again should take some pressure off. You won't have to worry that classes won't fill, and shows won't have to resort to fillers, which sometimes resulted in two-foot-six-inch Medal or Maclay classes!

When you get to the show, just do the best that you can. You need to give yourself a solid ride, so remember that you know your horse and you know that the questions that will be asked on a course are all ones that you can answer. You've done them all in your preparation.

Equitation courses are all formulas, so nothing should be a surprise. You practice the formulas at home. The questions asked will be about opening and closing the stride, doing rollback turns, angle jumps, skinny jumps with no standards—everything you've practiced in your lessons. The course is nothing more than a combination of these. So, when you get to a show, just remember how you did them at home. Say to yourself, "Yes, I did this at home so I can do it here at the show."

Keep your mind on those thoughts. If your mind goes other places, then *stop*. Turn it around and think of a positive ride you've had.

Instead of saying, "I'm not going to feel nervous" (which won't work), say "Okay, I feel nervous." Admit it. Then say, "Let me break this course down into segments." Think of similar segments at home where you had success. Take a deep breath and say, "There's nothing out there I can't answer." Thinking this way will empower you and enable you to give your horse the best possible ride.

Q. I have a horse at home for me and a pony for my eight year old daughter. She was very enthusiastic at first but seems to be losing interest. I really want to share riding with her. Do you have any idea how I can try to rekindle her passion that she once seemed to have?

A. See if there is a stable in your area that has a riding program geared to kids her age and level. If so, let them "play" with your daughter together with their ponies. Children her age love the social interaction with their peers. Kids who love their ponies will probably rekindle your daughter's enthusiasm.

If there's no local stable or not one that offers that kind of program, then see if there are other activities she might like to try. You might have to find your own riding "buddy" for a while. But don't push her to ride with you. Encourage her to explore other things she can do. She's still pretty young, and in time, she might want to come back to riding.

Q. I live in the Midwest, and both of my parents are well-known professionals. I love my horse and really enjoy riding him. But I really don't like showing anymore. The last few years, we've taken green ponies, made them up, sold them, and made a lot of money. Now my parents want to do this with horses. I'm afraid if I tell them I don't want to show, it will make them angry because this is how they make money. I really love my horse and want to ride, but how do I tell my parents I don't want to show anymore?

A. Okay, it's important that, as a child, you understand that you are not responsible for your family's income. If your parents are both professionals, I'm sure they'll figure out how to make money without you having to ride horses in shows. There are probably kids in your area who would *love* the chance to show green ponies and horses. With your parents' training expertise and ability to sell ponies they've brought along, I'm sure their business will be fine. But it's very important to tell them how you feel. They might be disappointed that you don't want to show anymore, but you're not responsible for their feelings. They will *not* be disappointed in you… though they might be disappointed that you don't want to "show" anymore. That's a *big* difference. Maybe in time you'll want to show again, and maybe you'll just enjoy riding because you love these wonderful animals. That's fine too! Kids and adults ride for all different reasons. Some people just want to ride because they love the feeling and excitement it gives them. I think you need to tell your parents what you want to do and know it's okay … and it is okay!

important event, I probably would just "hack" my horse and let him relax for a job well done.

Q. My trainer found me a horse a few years ago that I loved, although he certainly knew more than I did. I think that was a good thing! Then I moved to the west coast and began training with someone my trainer encouraged me to go to. Unfortunately, during a lesson, I fell off and was seriously hurt. My trainer thought my horse was way too much for me. So, we sent him back to the professional I'd bought him from. Now I'm back again on the east coast riding with the trainer whom I was with originally. When I had him on the east coast, he never put a foot wrong. Now every day I regret selling him. He was big, beautiful, and extremely comfortable. I don't know what happened on the west coast… or why I was thrown. I don't know if I'll ever have another horse like him. Right now, I have a wonderful schoolmaster whom I adore he's older and can only jump two feet six inches. He's really a wonderful school horse but not a show horse any longer. He'll never have another home. I'll retire him when he says he's had enough, but my goal is to have a horse I can show in the three-foot adult hunter division. How do I get over the grief I feel daily about having sold the horse I know could have taken me to my goal?

A. Well, I guess the best answer I can give you, is that if the professional, you're back riding with, found the horse you're grieving, I imagine she or he will be able to find you another horse. It's truly a shame your horse didn't work out on the west coast, but I imagine when you had your serious accident, it probably scared that pro half to death! Speaking from experience, teaching adults can be very challenging. My priority list goes as follows: first is safety. Adults don't bounce like kids. When they fall, there is much more chance of the adult getting hurt than a child. Also, adults usually have much more on their plate, for example, job, family, partner, husband, wife, kids, and so on. Second on my list is character. By character I mean a very steady temperament. I don't want a Jekyll/Hyde. I want the adult horse to ride pretty much the same all week. I don't want a horse that has to be lunged or ridden each time before the adult rides him. My third prerequisite the horse's size and shape. I'm pretty good at matching horse and rider. The last two priorities are the rider's goal and their budget.

If this professional whom you're back with found the horse you so desperately miss, it seems to me that he or she can find you another. I don't mean to dismiss your heartache, but after a serious fall, I'd be pretty reluctant to put you back on that horse too. Let that one rest and look forward to finding a new horse that you can develop a relationship with like the one you have with your wonderful schoolmaster.

Q. I'm an adult rider, and I had a very bad accident about six months ago. It was my mistake, not my horse's. I've just started jumping again, but I get *very* nervous when I'm heading to an oxer. All of a sudden, my mind goes back to my accident, and I end up pulling my horse up. I want to continue jumping, but neither my teacher nor I know how to fix this horrible problem. I don't want my horse to become a stopper. Any help will be greatly appreciated.???

A. It's extremely important to jump a lot of very small jumps to get your confidence back. I'd set up a trotting gymnastic where you'd trot in over a cross rail, then one easy stride to a small vertical and another easy stride to a small cross rail oxer. When you're comfortable, open the footage between the jumps and canter in over the exact same small jumps. Again, when you're comfortable, take away the cross rail and canter the vertical and cross rail oxer. When you're feeling confident, make the cross rail oxer into a small normal oxer. Then after a period of time, set up a related distance from the vertical to the oxer. When you're comfortable jumping in that one direction on both leads, then jump it going the other way, from oxer to vertical. You have to understand that your fear is real, and you have to go slowly to rebuild your confidence. Think of the tortoise and the hare story … which one got to the finish line first? You'll achieve your goal if you go back to jumping small fences, especially oxers, in various situations. The way the jumps are set can ask different questions, and you can increase the height and width as you gain more confidence. My main suggestion is to acknowledge your fear and take it slowly. You will be able to "get back" and regain your confidence.

Q. When I have a jumping lesson at home, I'm fine. When I'm in the schooling ring at a horse show before my class, again I'm fine. But when I'm at the in gate, I get so nervous I feel like I'm going to throw up. Any suggestions of how to handle my nerves?

A. Actually, it's a good thing! It means your adrenal system has kicked in, and it heightens your awareness. First, acknowledge your nerves, because right now your nerves are in control. The more you try and *not* feel nervous, the more nervous you'll become. Nervousness is a strong emotion and has a lot of energy. It's similar to actors in a live play… they often have butterflies. You have *killer bees*! So, here's your exercise. You're going to develop a friendship with three butterflies by giving them the first names of three of your friends. You're going to get this set up before you go to your show. Once at the show, you're going to ask your butterflies to hop on your shoulder and come ride with you in a horse show class. Now, I imagine you're giggling, laughing, or just thinking I'm completely crazy. But by doing this, you've just taken control of your emotions rather than having your emotions controlling you! I suggest that as you're walking to the ring or standing at the in gate, you talk very quietly to your butterflies; if you're too loud, or people will think you're "crazy". Go over the plan for your course with your butterflies, and this should put a smile on your face. Also, take some slow deep breaths; this will help oxygenize your body, which will help you think in the ring and relax too. However, now you'll be in charge of your emotions rather than having your emotions control you.

Q. When I rode as a junior, I was fearless, and I was very competitive in the junior jumper division at many of the "big shows". When I went to college, I had to sell my horses and stop riding, which was very hard to do. Now, many years later with an excellent job and a great fiancée, I've started riding again. But for the first time in my life, I'm finding I'm quite fearful. I don't know why, and I have no idea how to get "brave" again. Please help!

A. There are several issues and reasons you're feeling this way, and it all makes perfect sense. When we were kids, first of all, we thought we were immortal! As adults, we realize several truisms. One is we are *not* immortal! We have many more things on our plate than we did as juniors. We have jobs, many times partners, and when we fall, we don't "bounce" like we used to. If we fall off, there is a greater chance that we will get hurt. Remember, riding *is* an inherently dangerous sport. If we break something, it can possibly keep us away from our job for a (significant?) period of time. Unless you own your own company and/or you're your own boss, then he or she does not look favorably on an employee missing work due to a riding accident. So, your fear is actually a good emotion to have when you start back. It probably means you'll take things slowly. Know the feeling you're experiencing is a normal one, no matter how fearless you were as a kid. Give yourself time to get reacquainted and make sure the horses you're riding are safe and you're under someone's guidance whom you trust. I feel pretty confident that if you understand why you feel this way and you're willing to give yourself some time and have a horse that will be able to provide you safety and fun, you'll probably be able to set sensible goals and attain them. Good luck!

Q. I'm an adult and have ridden with the same trainer for the past five plus years. She's a wonderful person and a very good teacher, but I feel like I've kind of outgrown her, and I think it's time for me to move to another trainer. I don't want to hurt her feelings, but I think I'll continue to learn more from a different person. I'd be leaving a small business, and I know it will hurt her financially. I am so stressed with my decision, and I don't know how to handle this so I can leave on the best terms possible. Please help me???

A. This is a tough one. On the one hand, it sounds as though you've probably learned as much as you can from this teacher, and to continue your learning, it's time to move on. Yet you don't want to hurt her emotionally nor financially. However, remember you had different teachers from kindergarten through high school. Some teachers are wonderful teaching great basics to kids and adults and maybe wonderful taking kids and adults from short and long stirrups through children's and adult hunters and jumpers. But past the three foot division, you'll probably need another trainer who has more people in the barn doing three feet six inches classes. So, another trainer is more interested and qualified to teach junior and amateur jumpers. And lastly, another trainer that works with very accomplished horses and riders at the grand prix level. So, you see, it's a progression of teachers, similar to school without going to new teachers every year. Most trainers recognize their best niche but find it very difficult "to let go".

I'd suggest that you take her out to lunch or dinner and have this conversation with her. Let her know how hard this is for you and how much you've learned and grown from her. Let her know that this is a very hard decision, but you feel it's time to move on; however, you'd still like to be friends, if she's willing. Hopefully, financially she'll get some new clients at the stage you started with her. But you can't "control" her business, and if you stay because of that concern, you'll probably end up feeling resentful that she "kept" you there. Good luck with your move. I'm behind you on this one.

Q. I have a rider who has been doing the three-foot divisions successfully, and I feel she is ready to move up to the three-six classes. She is a bit nervous, and I would like to help her transition confidently. What suggestions do you have?

A. When you (the trainer) are thinking about moving your student to a higher, more advanced division, there are a few things you need to do to ensure a smooth transition. Equitation and jumper courses are a series of formulas that ask specific questions. It is important that riders are comfortable answering these questions at a lower height before advancing to higher divisions. You must also know that the horse will be comfortable jumping the higher height. Sometimes a horse is quite confident jumping three feet, but the additional six inches go past that horse's comfort zone. Both the horse and rider need to be capable of jumping a bigger track.

The rider needs to feel confident that she is not being over faced. Many riders when starting the more advanced division appear to rush the course. When you walk the course with your rider, segment the course and find places where she can regroup. Sometimes courses have a "fast track", but even these courses have places where riders can take a breath.

Remind your student that she has experienced these questions either at other shows at a lower height or at home in lessons. Be specific. You should never put your rider in a horse show situation that she has never experienced. There, of course, is a muddling time your rider goes through in answering all the questions asked in the advanced classes. This is normal and sometimes can be quite frustrating, but most riders go through this process.

It is important when your rider finishes her course that you discuss both the parts of the course that she rode well and how to improve the sections that need improvement. End your analysis on a positive note. Even when kids are riding very experienced horses, it usually takes time for them to feel comfortable and confident in a newer advanced division.

Stay positive in your approach. Your student, feeling your confidence, will rise to the occasion!

Q. My daughter is showing very successfully in the big eq and jumper divisions. She has decided she wants to become a professional, but she's not sure what is the best way to prepare herself. Could you give her some advice?

A. I think every young high school graduate should take advantage of a college education if financially possible. I suggest majoring in psychology or business. Both will be helpful in their equestrian pursuits. It also gives them choices in their lives.

However, if continuing school is neither an option nor an avenue to follow, then she or he should go to a professional and see if it's possible to be a working student, perhaps minimally paid. No matter how successful she was as a junior, she will start at the bottom of the "food chain". But it is a way to begin to understand all that goes into being a professional. She can amass a huge amount of information that she may not know. This includes lesson schedules, horse training schedules, feed, medication, setting up vanning, hotel reservations, horse show entries, barn insurance, payroll, workman's compensation, employee health benefits, and all the other intangibles that go into an operation

There are no more professionals who just ride. Riders are a dime a dozen. Even top jumper grand prix riders and our best hunter riders have to be able to teach or have such a large business that they have additional staff to do some of it. Many juniors can ride great but have no idea what it really takes to become a professional. It is a 24-7 job. There is little time for a "regular" life. It's a lot of hard work yet can be incredibly rewarding if you're willing to dedicate the time, effort, and energy.

It's not easy to get into the system, especially on either coast, other than the way I've mentioned. It might be a little easier to get your foot in the door in the Midwest or Southwest, where the areas are not so populated. Both coasts are so competitive it's hard to get into a well-known establishment. But again, I don't want to discourage her from trying. Just know it will require hard work, many hours, and determination to succeed.

CHAPTER 5

OTHER QUESTIONS

Q. I am looking for a "big equitation" horse for one of my students, and some people won't let me take horses out on trial. This is a huge investment, and we can't judge just by one or two rides at their farm. Do you have any suggestions so we can get a good feel of a horse when we are not allowed a trial period?

A. First, I suggest you only deal (work) with professionals whom you trust. When I am trying horses to be used in the equitation division, these are some of the questions I ask about the horse and look for. Is the horse's stride elastic? In other words, can the horse easily open and close its stride? Does the horse have scope? Is the horse attractive? Does the horse have a good "counting" canter? Is the horse smooth, both on the flat and over the jumps? Can the horse make all the distances (medium, a little short, a little long) all look effortless? Is the horse brave? The top equitation horses today have *all* the positive attributes of a low level (three feet six 2)inches to three feet nine inches) jumper, as well as the quality of today's hunter! It's not easy to find.

Then it depends on the size of your pocketbook. Both successful equitation horses and potentially the "up-and-coming" horse can and will be very expensive. Going to Europe, due to the Euro is not a good deal today. Look more locally or even in Canada. The Europeans have "caught on" to our hunter/ equitation business!

Here are several questions that you should ask the seller (not necessarily in this order), but get *all* these questions answered to your satisfaction: What are the horse's strong points? What are his weaknesses? Don't fall for the horse that is "perfect." *All* horses have strengths and weaknesses! Is the horse a good practice horse, as well as a good show horse? This is important if your rider needs to do homework to become more advanced. Some great show horses don't like to practice! What preparation does it take to get the horse to the show ring: lunging, morning exercise, lessons? What medications does the horse need, both at home and at the shows: joint supplements, Butazolidin, Banamine, Robaxin, and/or anything else? Has the horse been out of service for health or soundness issues?

Get the horse's show record. It's important to know if you are buying a horse from a well-known professional who has had the horse in his or her program for a period of time or if the horse is coming from a program that you think you can improve. Do you think you can improve the horse or hope to keep it up to its current level of competition? When you vet the horse, does it have issues that your vet thinks you can deal with in your stable management program?

All horses that have been actively showing will have "issues". You need to know whether you and your staff are capable of dealing with this horse's maintenance.

Q. What do pros' mean when they say, that when you ride, you're either training or untraining your horse"?

A. Horses learn by a process called conditioning. Through repetition, our aids become "hard wired" into our horses' brains. Pressure, whether It's from your hands, legs, spurs, or a stick, teaches our horses to react … it shapes their behavior. Relaxation of pressure is the horse's reward; it tells the horse he's done it correctly. I believe that horses learn on the reward or on the relaxation of the pressure used to create a reaction. This process is rehearsed over and over until a certain aid elicits a specific immediate, yet calm reaction. This is what we mean by "hard wiring" our horses to our aids. You certainly don't need to "train" your horse every time you ride. But understand, consistency of your program is *key*! For example, I probably wouldn't trail ride my horse the day before an important show or class, unless it was a *very* schooled horse, and I wanted to just give him a nice relaxing walk ride.

Q. Please explain the learning curve. I don't know how to help my riders when they get so frustrated?

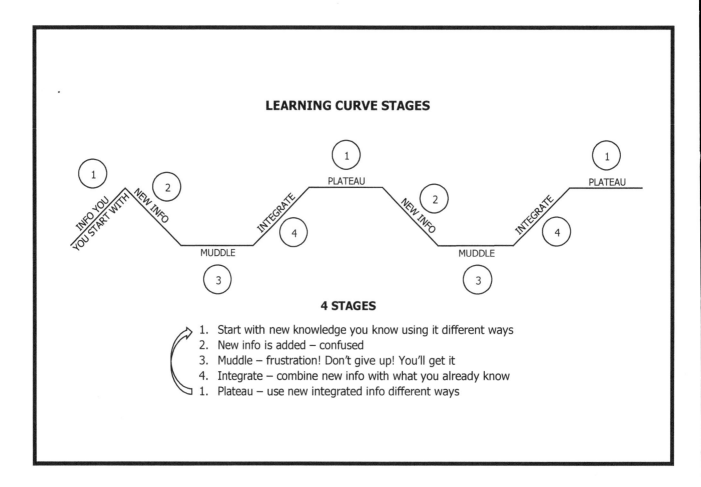

LEARNING CURVE STAGES

INFO YOU YOU START WITH | NEW INFO | INTEGRATE | PLATEAU | NEW INFO | INTEGRATE | PLATEAU

MUDDLE   MUDDLE

4 STAGES

1. Start with new knowledge you know using it different ways
2. New info is added – confused
3. Muddle – frustration! Don't give up! You'll get it
4. Integrate – combine new info with what you already know
1. Plateau – use new integrated info different ways

A. Starting off with a little information.

1. Plateau: This is where you the rider learns how to use the information he or she knows in many different ways. Like 7 + 3 = 10, 6 + 4 = 10, 2 + 8 = 10, and so on. Maybe this is where the rider learns how to use their calves, spurs, and stick reactive to their legs.

2. New information: This is hard to process and use with what you the rider knows. This leads to what I call the

3. muddling phase: This is when riders get very frustrated. They're just not getting it, and it seems the more they try to grasp it, the farther away "it" gets!

4. Integration: Now the new information begins to literally integrate with what they already know. It's like the *aha* experience! They get it!!! Then riders go back to step 1) the plateau ….

All riders go through these phases. There might be a handful of naturally talented people who go through this process much faster. But the only way I know to get through it faster is to have multiple horses, otherwise you just have to go through it. There is nothing you can do off your horse to get there faster that I know. In the forty or so years that I've been teaching, I've only had a handful of tremendously talented riders, yet I've had kids win all the equitation national championships and many Maclay regional championships. Some kids are very naturally talented… other kids, obviously with average talent, but have tremendous work ethics.

There are many learning stages… Think of the learning curve as a journey, not a sprint!

Q. I have a hard time remembering my equitation courses. This has never been a problem before now. All I can think about are my courses, so my rounds are a mess. Please tell me what I can do so I can remember my courses and have good rounds again.

A. Okay take a breath, because I have an easy solution for you. People have different modalities for learning. There are four learning styles: visual (seeing), auditory (hearing), kinesthetic (moving), and tactile (touching). You may have become more of a tactile learner.

I suggest that you go to the ring with a pad of paper and a pen or pencil. Write down the course by describing each jump in sequence. Let's say that the first jump, a vertical, has three red-and-white rails and two red flower boxes in front. Put a #1 in a circle next to your description, with an arrow indicating the direction you'll jump the fence. Then, just as specifically, describe the second fence, which might be an oxer, the same way again, and put a #2 in a circle with an arrow to indicate the direction. Continue to describe each remaining fence and its direction in the very same way.

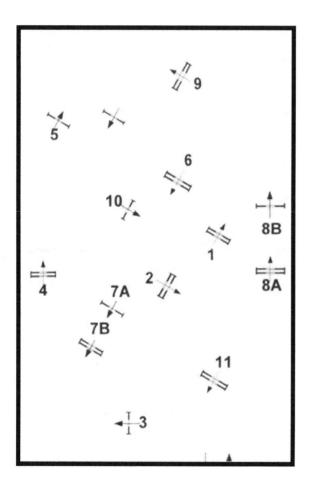

Once you're done, stand and look at the ring and tell yourself the course the very same way you wrote it down. Now fold your paper and put it in your pocket. Face away from the ring and tell yourself the course by describing each jump. Don't worry if you falter—just take the paper out of your pocket and rehearse the course again while keeping your back to the ring. Then put your paper back in your pocket and start again. Repeat the process until you know the course cold.

Just be convinced that this method will work. Take your time and keep your thoughts positive. This approach will take the pressure off remembering the course, and you'll be able to concentrate on your riding.

Q. How do I teach my riders to mount their horse correctly? They're a real mess when trying to mount. Thank you.

A: There are three ways to mount a horse correctly:

1. From a mounting block, a ladder, sometimes a jump
2. From the ground
3. By getting a leg up

Mounting in the first two ways are similar but with one slight difference. First, I'll explain mounting from a mounting block, a ladder, or a jump. Face *slightly* toward the back of the horse. The "off" rein (the outside rein the other side of the horse's neck) should be slightly shorter than the "near" rein (the inside rein closer to the rider). If the horse starts to move forward, he will move his front end away from the rider, but his haunches will travel toward you the rider so they can still get on. If the rider is holding a crop or stick, it should be carried in the left hand so as *not* to swing over the horse's back as the rider starts to go over to the other side. The rider starts by putting their left foot in the stirrup with their toe pointing into the girth, *not* in the horse's side. Then the rider puts their right hand on either the pommel (the front of the saddle) or the cantle (the back of the saddle) and their left hand on the mane. Then the rider swings their right leg over the horse. The rider should hold themselves up with their hands until they pick up the right stirrup and *gently* sink down into the saddle.

The only real difference when mounting from the ground is possibly lengthening the stirrup to get the left foot in the stirrup. Other than that, mounting is exactly the same.

The third way of mounting is by getting a leg up. For many years it was always done this way. But today I see more ladders, especially at horse shows. Obviously both the rider and the person giving the rider a leg up have to agree on the "number" when the rider is going to jump. By the way, the person giving the leg up is *not* a derrick (a large lifting device) but a "helper" to guide and "lightly" help lift the rider up. The rider should stand on the ball of her right foot and keep her ankle and knee joints supple so the leg up isn't dead weight. Her knee should be at about a ninety-degree angle. The reins and stick/crop should be held exactly the same way as with the first two methods. Once the "lift" begins, the rider puts her right hand on the pommel and left hand on the mane. Again, as the rider's right leg goes over the horse's back, she hold's herself up until both feet are in the stirrups; and again, the rider lowers her buttocks softly into the saddle.

Too many times I see riders just slam down into their saddle, and then they wonder why their horse doesn't stand still.

Q. I am an amateur adult who wants to do the adult hunters and perhaps amateur-owner hunters. I've shown successfully in both in the past. Unfortunately, most horses for these divisions are out of my price range, so I would like to get an off-the-track Thoroughbred and reschool him. Could you give me some advice on this process? I do have a good trainer to work with.

A. First of all, you're lucky to have a trainer who can deal with and school thoroughbreds. Most younger trainers today haven't been exposed to thoroughbreds but rather the warmbloods, which are more prevalent today.

Buying a horse off the track can be tricky. You need to ask several questions before purchasing a horse: Why is the horse for sale? Does the horse have any soundness issues? How is his attitude? Is the horse healthy? Is he for sale only because he was too slow for the track (the expression is, "a fat man could beat him up a hill")? Often a thoroughbred right off the track is very fit and needs a few months to be turned out in order to "decompress" from his track experience. Do you have the opportunity to see the horse walk, trot, and canter? Has he ever jumped? (Bear in mind that a horse jumped loose in a pen or a chute can jump very differently with a rider on its back.)

If you are satisfied with all of your questions being answered, then I would want to have a horse for a bit of time to see if he is capable of being transformed into a hunter/jumper. For the most part, thoroughbreds are more sensitive than warmbloods. Their training methods may be quite different depending on their mentality, personality, and development. They are usually quick to learn and maintain their lessons but need to be handled with more tact and encouragement. There is nothing better than a good thoroughbred, but you need to understand their sensitivity and their need to be handled differently than most warmbloods.

Q. I have a young horse I'm starting to work with that is wonderful under saddle. He is very willing and seems to really enjoy his job. But his ground manners leave a lot to be desired. He drags me around everywhere and won't stand still to be groomed or bathed. How do I teach him better ground manners?

A. It is imperative that your horse learns good ground manners. It's great that he is so good and kind when ridden, but you have to remember that he probably weighs somewhere between a thousand and twelve hundred pounds depending on his size and breed. You can get very seriously hurt if he does not learn to be a gentleman when you are working with him, whether it involves hand walking, grooming, washing, and/ or tacking.

What I'm about to tell you requires patience *and* firmness. When you hand-walk him, whether it's going to the paddock to turn out or walking him in hand after a ride, I suggest you use a chain lead shank and a leather halter. Begin by putting the chain through the lower ring on the halter and running the chain up across his nose and attaching it to the upper ring on the halter's off side. The reason I like to connect the chain to the upper ring is so the side piece of the leather halter does not interfere with his eye.

Practice walking and stopping him. He *must* stop at your side! If he does, give him a piece of carrot or candy and tell him he's a good boy. If he doesn't stop and drags you even a few steps, *smoothly* give a short (yet sharp) tug on the lead rope and say, "whoa." Once he stops, reward him. Repeat this exercise often. This is how horses learn…by repetition!

Once he understands his place is by your side and obeys your command to halt, then put on *another* lead rope just attached to the ring on the halter under his chin. Once he will stop by your side using just the shank under his chin, you no longer need the chain shank. But remember it is through consistent, patient repetition that your horse will learn.

I would use this same system in bathing him. Start with a chain shank over his nose and gradually add the shank just under his chin. When he understands what you want, he will be willing to listen to you and *not* walk all over you nor push you around.

As far as grooming, a lot of horses are ticklish or just have sensitive skin, especially under their belly, their sides, and flanks. Make sure your brushes are soft, even if it takes more time to groom him. If he's still unruly, put the chain shank over his nose and give him a smooth yet sharp jab and tell him *no*. When he stands politely, give him a treat.

Remember, we train disobedient horses by correcting their behavior through increasing pressure. When they behave, you reward them by decreasing that pressure. Horses are wonderful animals. Most try to please when they know what they are being asked to do and their program is consistent and fair.

Q. I'm concerned about whether my saddle fits correctly or not. Can you give me some pointers so I know if it's the right saddle for my horse, or tell me how I could go about finding a good saddle fitter?

A. I am not a ""saddle fitter", but I do think that saddle fitting has taken on a life of its own. Years ago, most people had one or, at most, two saddles and just put it on their horse(s). Now it seems as though we need to have a specific saddle fit a specific horse(s). I have a hard time with this concept! Just think of professionals who ride/show twelve to twenty horses daily. Do you really think they have that many saddles to fit all their horses? I don't think so.

Saddles, like other fads, become popular for a period of time until the next "better/or newer" saddle becomes the new fad. This has gone on for years. But if you want to buy a saddle to fit both a specific horse and you, these would be my recommendations.

1. Stand your horse on the aisle or a flat surface. Then put the saddle on your horse without a saddle pad. See if the saddle sits level; in other words, do the pommel and cantle sit evenly? One end of the saddle shouldn't sit higher or lower than the other.

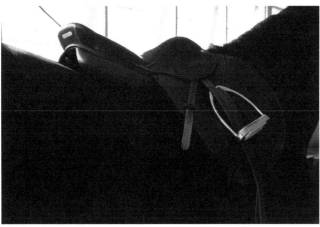

2. Make sure the saddle doesn't rock; (in other words, the saddle should sit "balanced" on your horse).

3. Make sure there is enough pommel room and that the gullet is wide enough for your horse's spine and that it doesn't pinch.

18)4. Make sure the front part of the saddle doesn't pinch your horse's shoulders. Your horse needs room to elevate and bring forward his shoulders to jump comfortably.

If you evaluate that these issues are comfortable for your horse, then you need to ride your horse to make sure you, too, are comfortable. If the saddle puts you in an awkward position, it may fit your horse but not you.

You might need to try several saddles to find the right fit for both you and your horse. Most tack shops have a person who will come out to your barn with several saddles to try and can usually help you find the right fit. Some tack shops will let you take a saddle home to try.

In my forty plus riding years, I have owned a grand total of four saddles! A sturdy and well-fitting saddle is a huge investment, but if you take care of your saddle well, it should last you for years and years.

Q. My trainer told me I need a stronger bit for my horse because he really leans on me. I've been using a D-ring snaffle. Could you give me a "Cliffs Notes" version of *Bits for Dummies* so I better understand the difference in bits and how they work?

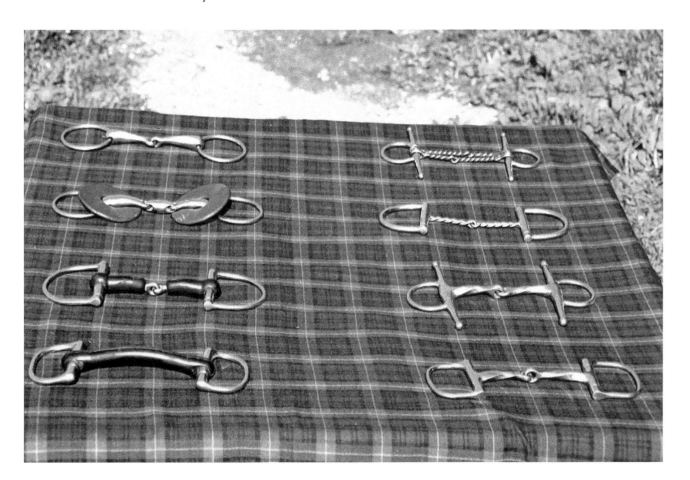

A. Bits work in four places in the horse's mouth: the corners (lips), tongue, roof, and the bars (area behind the front teeth, acting on the gums). The more sensitive areas are the roof and the bars. Conversely, the less sensitive areas are the corners and the tongue.

A bit with a curb chain works on a different area under the horse's chin. These bits include pelhams and kimberwicks.

When I am dealing with a horse that is heavy or pulls down, I go to a "mild" bit that works on the roof and the bars, rather than a stronger bit that works on the corners. I feel that stronger bits that work on the corners such as a sharp twisted snaffle, corkscrew, or twisted wire (single or double) ultimately create calluses, and the horse becomes deadened to the rider's hands.

A particular bit I like is the JP Korsteel Jointed snaffle. It is a "mild" port that breaks in the middle. As long as the horse stays light, the bit just rests on the corners and the tongue, but if the horse gets heavy or lugs, the bit reacts by going up into the roof and down to the bars. The moment the horse lightens up again, the bit goes back to the corners and the tongue.

If that is not enough to keep the horse light, I will go to a stronger port snaffle that has a hinge on both sides of the port. The higher the port, the more severe the bit. Ultimately, I might end up with a Segunda snaffle, which, in my opinion, is quite severe. A rider *must* have extremely educated hands to use this bit.

The bits I have mentioned are those that I would use for my hunters and equitation horses. Working with jumpers would take me in another direction.

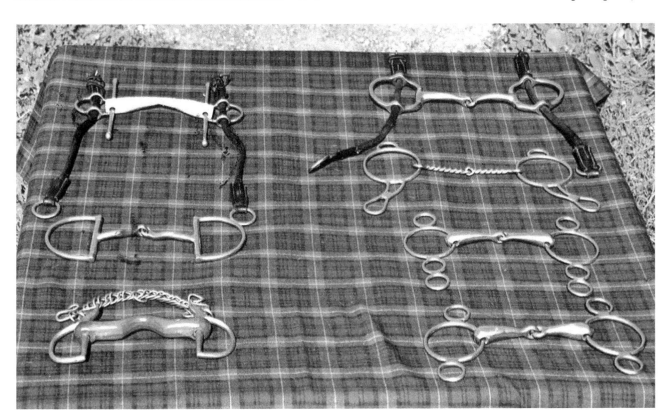

For jumpers that get heavy on the forehand, I would use a gag bit with either one or two reins depending on how much leverage I need. This bit will help lift the horse off his front end. These bits range from a rubber gag (straight or broken) to a loose ring gag, as well as a large variety of bits from soft to very severe bits. Again, it is important that the trainer understands how the different bits work, and whether the degree of education of the rider's hands is up to the job without punishing the horse.

Always remember that horses learn from the rider's reward, or relaxation of their aids. The correction or pressure creates the desired response, but the learning is accomplished through the "give". The stronger the bit, the more educated the rider's hands must be.

Q. I want to teach my horse to lunge. I have no idea how to start to train him to do this. We do have a round pen at the farm and I can probably use this to start him, if you think this a good way to start so he can't get away from me. He's pretty big and strong and he has a pretty high opinion of himself!

A. I suggest you use the round pen, not at first to lunge, but to acclimate him to these surroundings. I would take a bucket of grain, carrots, mints, or whatever he likes to eat. Use the food to encourage him to go into the pen with you. I would walk him into the round pen and just casually walk him around it. Then I would take him out and repeat this exercise several times until he becomes more confident. I would do the same thing over the next few days.

Once he is comfortable walking in the pen, then I would just let him loose to play. If you have the time, I would repeat this "playtime" for a few days. Let him understand that he can buck and play and happily go forward. Then I would bring in a lunge line and lunge whip. *Always have a lunge whip* even if you hold it down by your side. Start him in whichever direction he normally likes to go. The smaller the circle, the more control you'll have over him. Point the lunge whip towards his hindquarters to "send him forward." Pointing the whip at his hindquarters acts as your legs. Once he is going forward smoothly and quietly, point the whip toward his shoulders. This will keep him from coming in towards you; now the whip acts as your hands. If he slows down, point the whip toward his hindquarters so you actually go back and forth with the whip. Also, make sure you're *always* facing your horse. As he learns how to lunge, make his circle larger. If he becomes naughty, make the circle smaller.

If you are unable to do this yourself, then I would recommend you ask someone else to give you some help, so that neither you nor the young horse gets hurt.

Q. My eight-year-old gelding plays on the turns. He jumps great, has easy lead changes, is brave and honest, but he just loves to play and give little bucks on the turns. This behavior keeps us from getting good ribbons at the horse shows. He does this at home, too, but not as much as at the horse shows. What can I do?

A. That's great that he feels so good about himself! However, in the hunter/equitation ring, such exuberance is frowned upon. Since he does this at home, it makes it pretty easy to eliminate this behavior. When you are schooling him at home and he "plays" on the turns, you can do one of two things to eliminate his friskiness. If he is jubilant, make him trot in a circle and don't canter and approach the next jump until he is respectful and obedient to your aids.

Remember how horses learn: by a process called conditioning. He obviously enjoys jumping, so his reward is to continue on course, and his correction is to circle until he behaves himself. You must be consistent with this program even if you need to circle him in the show ring until he pays attention. If he really wants to continue jumping, this correction is the best method. He must be obedient, or he will not be allowed to continue jumping.

If his "playfulness" is more extreme, then halt him when he becomes too exuberant. Then make him circle until his behavior improves. The main thing is to eliminate this behavior at home and be willing to do the same at the horse show. I think once he's better mannered at home, he will be better in the show ring. If not, do the same in the ring. Don't correct him with your own emotion. Be very professional and very consistent in your approach to his problem. It should be easy to correct this behavior if you're willing to be consistent. That is the key!

Q. How do I find a legitimate trainer?

A. This is a really good question. Actually, quite honestly, I've never given this any thought. But it really required me to give a very thoughtful answer. I think you'd have to make a list to find the answers to the following questions

What are your goals?

How far are you willing to travel?

What level rider are you at this time?

Do you own your own horse? What if the trainer you're thinking about doesn't want your horse? Are you willing to buy a new one?

Do you want to be in a large barn? By that, I mean a trainer who has a lot of clients, with several assistants, or a small barn with a smaller clientele?

What credentials does this trainer have? What and who has he or she produced in the specific division(s) you're interested in?

You should definitely go to barns that you're interested in and have a scheduled meeting with the manager (or the head trainer). Walk through the aisles and look in the stalls. How do the stalls look? Are they clean? Do the stalls have enough shavings? Do they have clean and ample water buckets? Are the aisles clean? Do the aisles look safe? Are the wash stalls and grooming stations safe and clean? Is there proper ventilation throughout the barn (s).

Check out the footing in the different arenas.

Is the footing kept groomed and watered?

Do you know people who ride there? If so, get their input.

Can you ship in and take a lesson on your own horse? If not, do they have a horse you can take lessons on? Many barns don't have school horses. Especially in the Northeast because the overhead is just too expensive. If you can't take a lesson, then watch a few.

There are probably many more questions that are important to you. But I suggest you make a prioritized list. Then I think you'll find your answers and be able to make an informed, thoughtful decision.

Q. My horse has decided he really doesn't want to be a show hunter any longer. He gets very anxious and even feels fearful in the show ring. But when I'm home and take him for trail rides, he's wonderful. He's relaxed and jumps anything in front of him. I've had him checked by my vet, and he's both healthy and sound. We think he's just sour and has had his fill as a show horse. He's not that old, only thirteen. I think he'd make a great field hunter for a big man since he's a big horse, almost seventeen hands. He's very quiet and extremely comfortable to ride. How do I find out if this would be a good niche for him?

A. Your best bet would be to see if there is a recognized hunt somewhere near where you live. If so, find out who is the Master and give that person a call and explain your and your horse's situation. Maybe you could send a video, something very informal from your camera. Just so this person can decide whether it's worth a look. If the Master thinks your horse might work, depending on the hunt season (time of the year), he might want to take your horse on "trial" to see if your horse is comfortable with hounds and a group of horses. If so, this might be the right niche for your horse. The Master will be able to determine your horse's market value for this job.

If you "listen" to your horse, as apparently, you're trying to do, your horse will "tell" you what he or she would like to do. Then you can find the right job, so your horse has a good fit for a good life!

Q. I have a jumper that is very talented but sometimes he rears. I'm not sure how to handle it. I don't want to get rid of him because he's very talented. I'd just like to teach him not to do that! What suggestions do you have?

A. As always, my first question to you is if this is a new behavior? If it is, then I'd have your vet check his soundness and saddle fit. If he's uncomfortable, whether it be a slight lameness or the saddle pinching him and he is "acting out", then he may be acting this way because of discomfort. That could possibly be easily resolved.

If not, however, then you've got a real problem. No matter how talented your horse is, rearing is a *dangerous* vice! If he is physically sound, and there is no reason that you can think of for this behavior, and you want to try everything you can to try and make it work, I would send him to a cowboy or a pro who deals with this type of problem. I think horses that rear are dangerous. If you're intent on trying to resolve the problem yourself, then what you need to do is feel as soon as you "think" he might rear, and then crank his head towards your knee-either side, it doesn't matter. The horse's neck is its balance system. If his neck is pulled to one side, he cannot rear. But you've got to feel it and be quick!

I personally don't think a child, or an adult should try to correct rearing problems. This should be done by a professional who knows how to deal with this issue. Hopefully your horse can come around and be rid of this vice. If so, then you've got a nice talented horse. But I strongly suggest you get professional help with this problem. You could be playing with fire.

Q. How do I find the right pony for my child?

A. I think it's very important that you find a trainer you trust and have confidence in to find a pony for your child. Going out by yourself to find a pony to buy or lease is *extremely* risky!

It's difficult enough for professionals to find the right pony or horse. There are so many things to consider, including the pony's attitude, rideability, performance both under saddle and jumping, personality, compatibility, and price. I don't think parents can expect themselves to do enough due diligence to find the right pony.

So again, I strongly suggest that this parent put herself into the hands of a professional she trusts to find the right pony for her child.

Q. I took my daughter out of the barn where she was riding because the trainer there was not supportive. In fact, she could be pretty negative. My daughter shows a lot of potential, and I want to be sure to get her in a barn with a supportive trainer who will help her realize that potential. Could you give me an idea as to how I could go about finding the right fit?

A. I have a few suggestions that might be helpful in finding a more supportive trainer to teach your daughter. First, does she have friends who ride at other barns in your area? That could be very helpful. If so, perhaps she could "visit" them at their barns and watch some lessons. She'll probably get the best "feel" that way. Obviously, if she could have a riding lesson, that would be best, but that's not always possible.

Another thing you and she can do is go to a horse show, and stand by the schooling rings, and watch how trainers interact with their students. Then go to the show ring and stand by (unobtrusively), and again get a sense of how the pro talks to his or her students both before going into the ring and when the riders exit This should give you an idea of whether you like the interaction between the trainer and student.

Finally, set up a meeting with the potential trainer and discuss your daughter's goals and see if it looks like a good match. Also look at the facility. Does the staff seem competent? Are the stalls clean, and do they have good ventilation? What are the riding rings like? Is there turnout? Are there safety systems? And ask about any other concerns you will have for your horse's protection and safety.

Q. I have a really nice four-year-old that I want to keep sound and competitive for as long as possible. I see too many horses being pushed too hard too fast and disappearing from the show ring at a young age. How should I handle his career to best keep him sound?

A. This is an interesting question, for there are no "absolute" answers. I'm sure different professionals will have many different answers from their own experiences. For me, however, there are a few important questions you need to ask yourself:

How mature is his physical, mental, and emotional development? Most horses have not fully grown at four years. Is he still getting taller or just filling out?

Remember, horses were not put on this earth to be ridden over jumps. They are front weight-bearing animals. Their bodies need to be fairly developed to handle the stress jumps put on both their front and back ends. How does he handle new situations? Is he relaxed and confident in himself? How far along is his schooling? Does he do flying changes yet? How high has he been jumping? What will it take to prepare him to show? Will you need to lunge him or ride him an hour or so before the first class?

What are your long-term and short-term goals other than keeping him as sound as possible? Do you have a trainer or ground person to help you?

Only you and the trainer, if you have one, can answer these questions.

I always err on the side of being conservative. If you have a car/truck and trailer, I would take him to some shows and just school him or just ride him around the grounds and see how he copes with being away from his own barn and ring. This will give you information about his attitude and self-confidence. If and when he is relaxed in the new environment, I would go to a show that had a ticketed warm-up or a schooling show (not USEF). I would start at an unrecognized show since the fees will be lower. You will not have USEF fees and office fees, and usually, the entry fees are lower. Maybe go in some under saddle classes to see how he adjusts to other horses in a ring.

I hope you've both enjoyed and learned from the questions and answers in this book. These are MY answers from about fifty years of experience. There are many other "answers", these are the ones that have consistently worked best for me over time.

THE END

I'd especially like to thank my demonstrators for all the photos in my book. Both Kate Smith and Linda Giles were wonderful showing the correct way to answer the questions that were asked in this book.

I'd especially like to thank my demonstrators for all the photos in my book. Both Kate Smith and Linda Giles were wonderful showing the correct way to answer the questions that were asked in this book.

Thank you Judy Richter for the use of your wonderful Coker Farms in Bedford N.Y. for all the photos in this book. The ring, each day, was manicured and the jumps freshly painted. I sincerely appreciate your help for my first book.

CPSIA information can be obtained
at www.ICGtesting.com
Printed in the USA
BVHW022106110920
588351BV00010BA/224